The Republic

Plato

philosophy
in focus

The Republic
Plato

Jeremy Hayward
Daniel Cardinal
Gerald Jones

Academic consultant
Stella Sandford

Hodder Murray
A MEMBER OF THE HODDER HEADLINE GROUP

Authors

Jeremy Hayward is a lecturer at the Institute of Education, London; **Daniel Cardinal** is Head of Philosophy at Orpington College; **Gerald Jones** is Head of Humanities at the Mary Ward Centre, London.

The academic consultant **Stella Sandford** is Principal Lecturer in Philosophy at Middlesex University, London. Her most recent book is *How to Read Behaviour* (Granta, 2006).

Every effort has been made to trace all copyright holders, but if any have been inadvertently overlooked the Publishers will be pleased to make the necessary arrangements at the first opportunity.

Although every effort has been made to ensure that website addresses are correct at time of going to press, Hodder Murray cannot be held responsible for the content of any website mentioned in this book.

Hodder Headline's policy is to use papers that are natural, renewable and recyclable products and made from wood grown in sustainable forests. The logging and manufacturing processes are expected to conform to the environmental regulations of the country of origin.

Orders: please contact Bookpoint Ltd, 130 Milton Park, Abingdon, Oxon OX14 4SB. Telephone: +44 (0)1235 827720. Fax: +44 (0)1235 400454. Lines are open from 9.00a.m. to 5.00p.m., Monday to Saturday, with a 24-hour message answering service. Visit our website at www.hoddereducation.co.uk

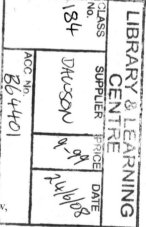

© Jeremy Hayward, Daniel Cardinal and Gerald Jones 2007
First published in 2007
by Hodder Murray, an imprint of Hodder Education,
a member of the Hodder Headline Group
338 Euston Road
London NW1 3BH

Impression number 10 9 8 7 6 5 4 3 2 1
Year 2011 2010 2009 2008 2007

Artwork by Art Construction, Tony Randell, Richard Duszczak
Cover design by John Townson/Creation
Cover photo © Archivo Iconografico, S.A./Corbis
Typeset in 11/13 Galliard by Dorchester Typesetting Group Ltd, Dorchester, Dorset
Printed in Malta

A catalogue record for this title is available from the British Library

ISBN-10: 0 340 88803 2
ISBN-13: 978 0 340 88803 2

Contents

Key to features

ACTIVITY — A practical task to help you to understand Plato's ideas.

▶ criticism ◀ — Highlights and evaluates some of the difficulties Plato faced.

experimenting with ideas — Plays around with some of the concepts discussed; looks at them from different angles.

A direct quotation from Plato's writing.

⚠ **more difficult** — A more in-depth discussion of Plato's work.

Read the Republic pages — Highlights the key pages of the *Republic* that you should read before continuing with this book.

The series

This series is for students who are beginning to study philosophy. The books fill the middle ground between introductory texts, which do not always provide enough detail to help students with their essays and examinations, and more advanced academic texts which are often too complex for students new to philosophy to understand.

All of the study guides are written around the themes and texts for the AQA AS level philosophy specification. In addition to Plato's *Republic* there are five other guides available:

- *Moral Philosophy: A Guide to Ethical Theory*
- Descartes' *Meditations*
- Sartre's *Existentialism and Humanism*
- *Epistemology: the Theory of Knowledge*
- *Philosophy of Religion*

The authors have substantial experience of teaching philosophy at A level. They are also committed to making philosophy as accessible and engaging as possible. The study guides contain exercises to help students to grasp in a meaningful way the philosophical theories and ideas that they'll face.

Feedback and comments on these study guides would be welcome.

Notes on the text

This book is intended as a companion to Plato's *Republic*. The book focuses primarily on the section from Book 5, 474c to Book 7, 521b and we suggest that this book be read alongside these sections of the *Republic*.

All references are to the Penguin Classics 2003 edition of the *Republic* by Plato (ISBN 9780140449143), translated by Desmond Lee.

Words in SMALL CAPITALS are defined in the glossary on pages 175–177.

Introduction

The influence of Plato's *Republic* runs deep, not just within philosophy, but through many branches of the history of European ideas, including the religious doctrines of Christianity and the theological reflections of its practitioners, theories of education, aesthetics, psychology, sociology and politics. The *Republic* is Plato's most famous book, and for good reason: the scope of the topics it covers is truly remarkable. It begins with the moral and political question of what justice is, but the inquiry quickly pans out and by the end of the book Plato has outlined his Utopia or ideal state, given a critique of various forms of government including democracy, explained how we should be educated and considered the place of women in society. However, the inquiry goes beyond purely social and political questions; it outlines Plato's views on the value of poetry and art, the ultimate nature of reality, what genuine knowledge is and how it is to be acquired, as well as the nature of the human soul and of life after death.

Our aim in this book is to look at Plato's exploration of all these themes, while focusing on the best-known section of the *Republic*, from Book 5, 474c to Book 7, 521b, where Plato is particularly concerned with his exploration of the nature of genuine philosophers and the knowledge they seek in order to argue that it is they rather than the people who should govern his ideal state.

The *Republic* is traditionally divided into ten books, although it is doubtful that Plato intended this, and these divisions seem to be the result of the length of available papyrus in ancient Greece.[1] There is also a convention that references to the *Republic* are taken from the pages of the sixteenth-century edition of the *Republic* by Stephanus. These references have been adopted by most translations and publications of the *Republic*, and we use them here.

The world has changed considerably since Plato wrote the *Republic* and many readers will be unfamiliar with the ancient Greek civilisation that forms the context out of which it appeared. To help in this regard, the first chapter provides some background information on Greek philosophy generally and Plato in particular and so the discussion of the text does not begin until Chapter 2. Those more familiar with the work of Plato may wish to start at that point.

Chapter 2 provides an overview of the *Republic* and the analysis of the text from Chapters 3 to 8 follows the order in which Plato presents the ideas from 474c to 521b rather than dealing with the different philosophical themes in turn. Although this latter approach would have the advantage of allowing a discrete and full exploration of the themes dealt with by Plato, part of our purpose here has been to allow the reader to use this book alongside Plato's text. By exploring the ideas in the order in which Plato himself develops them the reader may read this book without needing to jump back and forth within the *Republic*. At the same time, however, where necessary for a complete understanding of Plato's intention at any stage, we have engaged in lengthier analyses that incorporate ideas from different passages.

1

Background to Greek philosophy and Plato

Introduction

Plato is one of earliest philosophers in the western tradition and the first to leave behind a substantial body of text. Since only fragments of the writings of the thinkers who predate Plato have survived, it is tempting to imagine that all his ideas are original to him. However, examination of the evidence shows that in reality Plato was deeply influenced by certain key thinkers and it will be worthwhile examining what he learned from those who came before him. Before we turn to these influences, though, we should first briefly explore the cultural and social context in which these early Greek philosophers lived.

This chapter contains the following main sections:

■ Background to Greek philosophy
■ Background to Plato.

Background to Greek philosophy

Ancient Greece

The standard political grouping in modern times is the country, or nation state. Ancient Greece, however, was not a nation in the modern sense. Rather it consisted of a series of settlements, each with its own government and customs. Indeed there were several 'Greek' settlements in what we would now call Italy. Although often at war with each other, these separate groupings were united by a common language, religion and shared history – albeit with wide variations in all three. Each of these settlements would have a central stronghold which the inhabitants could fall back to and defend in times of attack. The term *polis* initially referred to these defensive areas (in Athens this was the Acro*polis*, on top of a large hill). However, in time the term *polis* came to refer to the whole settlement or city state.

Most of the city states were quite small, consisting of a few hundred families. However, a few, such as Sparta, Corinth and Athens, grew much larger and controlled large amounts of territory. With the expansion of industry and commerce, these states developed, and the wealthier citizens acquired slaves, often from prisoners captured in war. At the same time came the great outpouring of intellectual and artistic endeavour in mathematics, science, philosophy, architecture, poetry and drama that ancient Greece is famous for.

As the Greek city states grew, so did their importance in the western world. From the first Olympics in 776 BC through to conquests of Alexander the Great around 330 BC, Greek civilisation was the dominant force in the west. The height of Greek civilisation – its 'golden age' – is considered to be around 450 BC when Athens was under the influence of the statesman Pericles. Under the stewardship of Pericles – who had received extensive training in philosophy – Athens erected many of its famous buildings and refined its system of democracy. It is important to note that the rule of Pericles came just before the era of Plato; as a consequence, many of Plato's fellow Athenians were rather nostalgic and looked back to former 'glory' days. This nostalgia was just one of the factors leading to the moral crisis in Athens described below. The fact that in Plato's day the power of Athens was waning somewhat, and that other city states such as Sparta were on the rise, would have led many Athenians to ask questions about the correct way to organise a city; and the *Republic* itself grew out of such questioning.

The Greek civilisation continued to flourish after Plato's time; its dominance in the west came to an end with the rise of the Roman Empire from 300 BC onwards.

In terms of the written word the first texts to emerge from the ancient Greek culture were Homer's *Iliad* and *Odyssey* (see page 12) around 800 BC. From this point on, a wealth of poetry, philosophy and drama emerged.

Greek philosophy – the Pre-Socratics

The earliest writings that are recognisably philosophical involve a blend of philosophical and scientific speculations written in verse. Verse, as exemplified by the Homeric poems, was the only established form of writing at the time, so it is unsurprising that these early thinkers would adopt it to record and communicate their teachings. However, this can make interpretation of these early writings a difficult task, and one compounded by the fact that only fragments of the texts have survived. The philosophers who predated Plato, or more accurately predated Socrates, Plato's teacher, are known collectively as the PRE-SOCRATICS or sometimes the 'philosopher poets'. Naturally Plato was influenced by Pre-

Socratic thought, so it is worth briefly looking at a few of the key thinkers that helped to shape his philosophy. We will explore three in particular: Pythagoras, Heraclitus and Zeno.

Pythagoras

It is known that Plato spent some time living with Pythagorean thinkers, and this period is thought to have been instrumental in the development of his later THEORY OF 'IDEAS' or 'FORMS' (see below pages 68–84). Pythagoras (*c.* 570 BC–500 BC) was a philosopher, mathematician and general eccentric. He was gripped by numbers and geometric shapes, and particularly struck by the timeless nature of mathematical truths. For example, I might tell you that Margaret Thatcher was the Prime Minister and if you asked 'when?', I could give you the dates: between 1979 and 1990. But if I were to say that 4 + 3 = 7 then asking 'when?' would be nonsensical. There is no particular time when this sum is true. If four and three equal seven today, then they must always have equalled seven, and they always will. Truths like this don't go out of date. And yet all claims about the physical world, no matter how enduring, will one day cease to be true. All Prime Ministers will eventually be forced from office. Great oceans will one day turn to desert and great mountains crumble. Even the fact that the earth orbits the sun will one day cease to be.

Pythagoras was also struck with the idea that mathematical and geometric concepts, such as that of a triangle, do not concern just this or that triangle, but seem rather to be about some 'ideal' triangle which the mind apprehends. Thus, the concept of a perfectly straight line or a perfect circle is an idea which we can all understand quite well in our heads even though no one is able to draw a particular line that is truly straight or a completely perfect circle. Indeed, we seem able to have the idea of such things, even if we have never actually seen one in physical reality. Numbers too seem to be objects we comprehend with the mind rather than the senses. After all, you have never seen the number 3. Sure, we encounter physical objects in threes all the time, but never the 'threeness' itself that these objects instantiate. The number itself is an idea or ideal comprehended by the mind.

This way of thinking leads naturally to the idea that the world of mathematical objects is superior to the ordinary EMPIRICAL world of SENSE EXPERIENCE. Physical reality only ever contains imperfect circles, but our mind is able to contemplate and acquire certain knowledge of the ideal circle. And yet Pythagoras thought that these idealised numbers and shapes underpin and explain physical reality and therefore that a genuine understanding of the world is to be sought through an understanding of mathematics. He applied this way of thinking to the study of music. If you take any length of string, tighten and pluck it, it will produce a note. If you divide the length of string exactly in two and pluck again you will hear the same note, but exactly an octave higher. Divide the string again and this will happen once more and so on. What this example shows is that simple mathematics reflects the way an aspect of the world that we perceive works. And Pythagoras saw this as an example of a general principle, namely that, to gain a true understanding of any aspect of the world, it is necessary to seek out the mathematical principles that lie underneath it since the underlying reality of the world is mathematical.

■ **Figure 1.1**
Pythagoras believed that a mathematical reality underpinned the world we perceive

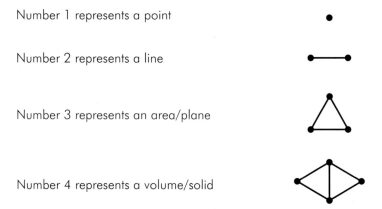

Number 1 represents a point

Number 2 represents a line

Number 3 represents an area/plane

Number 4 represents a volume/solid

Pythagoras is drawing a distinction between two worlds. There is a world of appearances, the physical world we see around us; but there is also a SUPERSENSIBLE reality, that is, one that the senses cannot perceive but which is recognised by the mind. But the world we perceive around us is not totally illusory and incomprehensible. Rather it is to be understood through a study of numbers and shapes, for mathematics and geometry provide the key to explaining the changing world of appearances. As we shall see, Pythagorean ideas find currency in Plato's writings. Notably Plato follows Pythagoras in his regard for the status of mathematics; he draws a very similar distinction between the real world apprehended by the mind and the apparent world of sense experience; and of particular importance to Plato was the idea that the philosopher's task is to use reason to uncover the reality that lies behind appearances.

■ Heraclitus

Second, there is Heraclitus (*c.* 540 BC–*c.* 480 BC). Like most of the Pre-Socratic philosophers, only fragments of Heraclitus' writings survive, and these fragments themselves make puzzling reading. He argued that everything was ultimately made of fire and that the state of the universe is one of conflict between opposites. Closely associated with these ideas is his best-known claim, namely that the world is in a state of perpetual flux – meaning that everything is constantly changing from one moment to the next. Objects become hot then cool down, trees grow then die, and the wind blows then is still. Everything is in a continual process of becoming something else – that is, what it is not – and so nothing can remain what it is from one moment to the next. A consequence of Heraclitus' view of the world is that it cannot be a proper object of knowledge. For since nothing in the world remains the same, nothing can ever be grasped by the mind before it has gone again. It is as though nothing in the world is still enough for us to take a mental photograph that could count as knowledge. Any snapshot will already be false as soon as it is taken. Plato takes seriously Heraclitus' claim that knowledge must be impossible of what is constantly changing and so agrees that we cannot have genuine knowledge of the physical world. But the real importance of this idea, for Plato, lies in his efforts to refute the conclusion that there can be no genuine knowledge. Following Pythagoras, this means that knowledge has to be of what truly is, i.e. the everlasting world which underpins physical reality.

■ Zeno

Zeno (490 BC–425 BC) explored many of the same themes as his mentor Parmenides (together they are known as the Eleatics because they came from Elea in southern Italy). One of the key problems that concerned all of the Pre-Socratics was the concept of *change*. How is it, they wondered, that something can change and yet be the same thing? Zeno, in particular, thought the very idea that change occurs was contrary to reason. To prove this point he devised several paradoxes to show that the concept of change is logically incoherent. One of the best known is that of the hare and the tortoise, which is adapted below:

Imagine a hare and a tortoise set off for a race. For the purposes of this story imagine that the hare is 10 times quicker than the tortoise and that, once started, they move at a constant pace. To make for a more sporting contest the hare agrees to allow the tortoise a small head start. The hare does not set off until the tortoise reaches the big tree in the road.

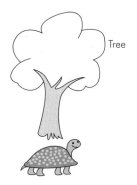

As the hare waits for the tortoise to reach the tree he begins to consider his race tactics. He reasons that to catch up with the tortoise he has first to get to the tree; and once at the tree, he thinks, he will take stock of the situation and set himself a new target.

The hare sets off and soon reaches the tree and, without stopping, looks up. The tortoise has made slow but steady progress and is now by a pretty flower a little further along the road. The hare again reasons that in order to catch up with the tortoise he has to at least get to the flower where the tortoise currently is. Once there he will set himself a new target.

■ **Figure 1.4**

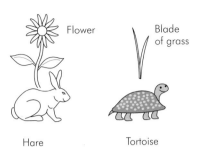

Pretty soon the hare reaches the flower and, without stopping, looks up. The tortoise has made slow but steady progress and is now by a blade of grass. The hare again reasons that in order to catch up with the tortoise he has first to get to the blade of grass where the tortoise currently is. Once there he will set himself a new target.

As the two are now very close, we will magnify their positions to make the situation clearer. It will resemble something like this:

■ **Figure 1.5**

But wait a second, isn't this just like the first diagram above? And if this is so couldn't we just substitute the tree for the blade of grass and repeat the diagrams all over again? It seems we are no closer to discovering the moment when the hare will actually catch the tortoise. We are stuck in a loop.

The three propositions below summarise our predicament.

A For the hare to catch the tortoise, the hare must at least pass the point where the tortoise currently is.
B It will take some time for the hare to reach that point.
C When the hare has reached that point the tortoise, who is moving constantly, will have moved on to a new point. And so we can move back to A.

It is difficult to see which one of these three propositions is false. But if they are all true then it would seem to be impossible for the hare to catch the tortoise.

Yet we see such events occur every day, not necessarily hares catching tortoises, but more likely one car overtaking another, or a bicycle passing a pedestrian. So it seems that on the one hand reason tells us it is impossible for the hare to catch up with the tortoise, yet on the other hand our senses tell us that hares catch up with tortoises every day.

So convinced was Zeno by his argument that he concluded that reason rather than the evidence of everyday experience was correct. Hares just cannot catch up with tortoises and so all movement, indeed any change at all, is impossible. What we experience with our senses must therefore be some kind of illusion. In the real world, the reality discovered by reason, nothing changes. In this way Zeno puts forward a dual world view: a world of change revealed by the senses, which is a mere appearance, and an unchanging truer reality revealed to us by reason.[2]

ACTIVITY

1 How is it possible for the hare to catch the tortoise?

2 Are any of A, B or C above false?

3 Do you believe that your senses deceive you in relation to objects catching up and passing one another?

4 What do you think Zeno concluded from this paradox of reason versus senses?

We see here the recurrence of a familiar Pythagorean theme and one which may seem very alien to the modern reader. However, at core it is not just one of the oldest but also one of the most enduring of philosophical ideas and in other guises should be pretty familiar. For many religions teach something very similar to this: they teach that the physical world we perceive around us is somehow illusory, imperfect or corrupt. This world is, in other words, not fully real. By contrast there is another world (for example, heaven) that is unchanging, eternal and perfect and which, with effort, we can hope to reach. This TWO-WORLD view, as we have suggested, will feature strongly in the philosophy of Plato as we shall see below, particularly when discussing his theory of Forms.

That ends our very brief tour of some of the philosophical ideas that were present before Socrates. Although Plato's philosophy can be approached with no prior knowledge, understanding the conceptual world he lived in can help to make sense of his thoughts.

In sum we've seen Zeno argue that our perception of the physical world of change is an illusion and that the real unchanging world lies beyond what we can sense. From Heraclitus we have learned that the world we experience is in constant flux and so cannot be known. And from Pythagoras we have the idea that the eternal truths of mathematics underpin and explain the world of the senses. It is from considering these and other ideas that Plato put together his theory of Forms (see page 68). This is the idea that there is an eternal, unchanging world, consisting of pure ideas or essences, contrasting with the world of change that we see all around us.

Athens in moral crisis

The *Republic*, like many of Plato's other dialogues, is concerned with moral questions or ethics. So, before approaching any of these works, it will be helpful briefly to explore the nature of moral thinking in ancient Athens in Plato's time. Morality is broadly concerned with the issue of how one should live one's life and how one ought to act. Ethical thinking involves engaging with very general questions about human conduct such as whether a person should seek pleasure, knowledge or try to help others; and also very specific and down-to-earth questions, such as whether to buy fair-trade tea bags if they are twice the price of ordinary ones.

Now, it is notable that the answers given to questions like these may be different from one person to another. While you may think it is OK to eat meat, someone else may judge it to be morally unacceptable. And even where there is general agreement in society on specific issues, we know that other societies have very different attitudes. For example, in contemporary Europe it is the norm to have just one husband or wife, while in other cultures polygamy and polyandry are accepted. We also know that thinking on certain moral issues has changed enormously over time. It used to be acceptable to use children as cheap labour, whereas this is now considered wrong. And sex outside of marriage was considered immoral until recent times.

When reading Plato we are given the opportunity to glimpse at the moral thinking of our distant ancestors. So if you think your grandparents approach moral issues in a different way from you, imagine how your great,

great, great grandparents would have thought. And yet what is striking is just how up to date much of Plato's thinking is. However, unsurprisingly, there are also important differences in the way the Greeks thought. Some differences are conceptually easy to grasp, for example women were not allowed to vote in ancient Greece whereas, in most societies, now both men and women may vote. Other differences are more challenging to make sense of.

The ancient Greeks had a conception of ethics far removed from our own and they did not have many of the moral concepts we have – for example, our own moral culture has been heavily influenced by religious notions of DUTY and obligation, and by political notions of RIGHTS, concepts which did not exist in Greek society. In recent times we tend to focus on specific *actions* when considering moral questions, for example, we might wonder whether it is right to experiment with genetically modified crops, or for doctors to perform euthanasia. But in Greek society moral discussion tended rather to address the question of what sort of person one should be. It was the person who was labelled as good or bad, rather than the action. The two approaches are of course linked. After all, we tend to judge someone who regularly performs bad actions as a bad person, and we tend to suppose that a bad person will perform bad actions. Nonetheless we can discern this difference in focus between Ancient Greek thinking and our own and so when looking at early Greek society we should not ask what *actions* did the Greeks consider good or bad, but rather what sort of *people* did they consider good and bad.

To answer this question, we will briefly go back to the beginning of recorded Greek thought – Homer.

Homer and Greek ethics

In about 800 BC, Homer wrote the *Odyssey* about the warrior Odysseus' journey back from the Trojan wars to his island home of Ithaca. Homer's writings are the first written records of Greek civilisation. His verses are steeped in the ideas and attitudes of his time and presumably reflect the way that people had thought for some time before. One important element of this way of thinking is reflected in Homer's use of the term GOOD (*agathon*). Early Greek society tended to reserve this term for noblemen or kings, but anyone in Greek society would be praised and blamed according to how well they carried out their allotted role in society. So, to be a good nobleman (not merely an ordinary nobleman), you must be brave, skilful and successful in war and in peace, have money, good looks and intelligence. These outstanding qualities were called 'excellences' or 'VIRTUES'. To be a good wife would be to perform your wifely role successfully, and this would involve, among other things, the virtue of being faithful; to be a good warrior would be to be athletic, accomplished in the arts of combat and fearsome in battle; to be a good farmer would be to possess those virtues required to farm well, and so on. So the concept of goodness or virtue was related to function, much like the way we now use the word 'good' in a non-moral sense. For instance, when describing a tin-opener as 'good' we mean it performs its function of opening tins well; and a good shower is one that produces lots of hot water.

To highlight the contrast between this Greek conception of 'good' and our own, take an example from Homer, from the *Iliad*. Hector kills Achilles' friend in a battle and so Achilles goes to avenge his death. Having killed Hector he drags the body daily round and round the tomb of his friend, then leaves it to be mutilated by dogs at night. The gods are horrified and hold a council at which Apollo, the enemy of Achilles, says 'Let him be aware lest we become angry, even though he is good.' What appears odd to the modern reader about this remark is why Apollo can still regard Achilles as 'good' after what he has done.

For each of the following things explain what would make it a good thing and give reasons why.

For example, a good chair is one that doesn't collapse when you sit on it, or destroy your back – in fact it facilitates the comfortable seated posture of the human body.

What makes a good…

…cook?

…film?

…action?

…person?

…life?

As we have seen, in ancient Greece, you were judged to be good (or not) according to whether you carried out your allotted social function in the appropriate way. This means possessing the necessary qualities to be a good warrior, nobleman, statesman, farmer, craftsman, etc. So for the Ancient Greeks there *was* a similarity between being a good tin-opener and being a good nobleman: you fulfilled your function (*ergon*), and did so in an excellent way. Now, this does not mean that they had no concept of blame: Achilles *ought* to have been righteous and obeyed the rules of the gods – so he *is* blameworthy even though his character remains good. So for Homer you can be good and still be blamed and punished for an action. In other words praise and blame are apportioned independently of being judged a good or bad person. To be good was still to be *enviable*, but this need not mean that one's actions were always praiseworthy. A good nobleman can use his virtues to perform blameworthy deeds. Judeo-Christian culture, by contrast, does not really distinguish between being praised or blamed for one's actions and being a good or a bad person.

Homer wrote of a time when society was fairly stable and had a pretty rigid hierarchical structure. By and large, a man would enter the same profession as his father and live in the same place, and things had been this way for a long time. In such an ordered society the idea of a good person being one who fulfils their allotted role or function in life makes sense.

However, after Homer, Greek society started to develop and flourish. The greater wealth that was produced and the increased social mobility eroded this traditional and ordered way of life. As the social order evolved, so the concept of what it was to live a good life also changed. As Greece became more economically successful, city states grew and social migration started to occur. What this meant was that people no longer simply lived the life they had been born into; rather, increasingly they would enter different professions and adopt new roles. This made it much harder safely to judge whether a person was fulfilling their function. The days in which everyone knew their place and their function were gone; for the new type of citizen might have several functions. In the five centuries that followed Homer, Greek culture underwent a crisis of confidence and, by the time of Plato, Homer's moral certainty had vanished and many of Homer's ideals were outdated. In particular the sort of excellences that Homer emphasised in his warrior-heroes such as Odysseus were no longer appropriate within the more complex society that had evolved.

At the same time as the small city states expanded, they came increasingly into contact with other cultures – Persian, Etruscan, Egyptian – which had different notions of what was good, and the Greeks came to recognise that their concept of good was not the only one. By the fifth century BC the moral conservatives in Athens, who harked back to Homer's day as a golden age of morality, were in a minority and unpopular. Athens entered a period of moral crisis in which it was no longer clear what being a good person involved.

The sophists

During this moral crisis a new breed of wise man came to the fore (480–380 BC). These new teachers would give lectures (for money) and educate young noblemen. Collectively they were known as the SOPHISTS (meaning 'wise men'). The sophists were usually widely travelled, and as they moved from city to city they witnessed at first hand how the values and customs of each Greek city state differed. What was prized in Sparta might well be rejected in Athens. Consequently, many of the sophists did not believe that moral questions had definitive answers. So while different sophists had their own philosophies, a common theme was a tendency towards MORAL RELATIVISM: that is, they were generally suspicious of the idea of any universal or objective moral truths. They appear to have regarded moral attitudes as a simple matter of the conventions of each city state. This means that what is considered good or bad is relative to the society you live in. It appeared to follow from this relativism that being successful within one's society was all one ought to aspire to, and the skills to achieve this could, they claimed, be taught. To be socially successful you needed to:

a) know the rules and conventions of the city state you lived in, and

b) know how to be persuasive in public debate.

The sophists said they could teach the art of debate and persuasion that would bring social standing and political power, and so inevitably they were very popular in the market places where they taught.

Moral and cultural relativism

Read the numbered statements and decide which of A, B, C below applies.

A   This is not true at all.
B   This is true only in a particular culture or cultures.
C   This is true in any culture.

1 The chemical composition of water is H_2O.
2 It is correct to drive on the left-hand side of the road.
3 Thin people are more beautiful.
4 All vixens are foxes.
5 Murder is wrong.
6 Hanging people is wrong.
7 It is wrong to have more than one husband or wife at a time.
8 Stealing is wrong.
9 Women should have equal rights to men.

Most people would claim C for 1 and 4: number 1 is a descriptive sentence and number 4 is true by definition. The rest of the statements involve some sort of VALUE JUDGEMENT about the world and here the situation regarding truth is less clear. Moral OBJECTIVISTS argue that moral truths are independent of the society that forms them. On this view if an action is morally wrong then it will be morally wrong for anyone, in all times and all places and regardless of the culture you happen to come from. Moral relativists on the other hand claim that the truth of value judgements depends on each culture and that there is no objective truth on such issues.

During the moral crisis in ancient Greece no one was sure how to be a good, virtuous person, for the meanings of the words seemed to have changed: the older generation wanted a return to the values expressed by Homer; the younger generation were ready for change. So, instead of teaching young men to be virtuous (which was expected of them), the sophists would teach them how to become successful, feeling that this was more important than trying to live up to outmoded concepts of virtue.

Teaching young men to be successful consisted of teaching them to speak well in public and thus know the popular line to take in front of a particular audience. In other words the sophists taught how to be popular and how to tap into public opinion, without actually teaching any moral convictions. Because of this the sophists have been compared to the spin-doctors of today, although, in their defence, they were quite a popular group within Greek society.

Summary of influences

From the snapshot above we can see just a few of the ideas that Plato would have been exposed to during the formative years of his life. We are not denying that Plato's ideas are themselves original, however; as with all ideas, they can naturally be seen as extensions and derivations of prior thinking.

The early Greek philosophers were interested in broad philosophical questions concerning the nature of reality. For example, is change possible? How can an object change yet be the same? Is there another reality? The sophists, by and large, were concerned with moral questions, no doubt reflecting some of the moral doubts of the times they lived in.

Plato's theory of Forms, which underlies much of the argument in the *Republic*, is a theory that addresses both these areas of concern. The theory attempts to answer questions about the nature of reality and in doing so provides answers to questions about how we gain knowledge. The theory also suggests that the highest Form of knowledge is knowledge of what is good. Plato suggests that there *is* a definite answer to all moral issues (although he does not actually tell us what these answers are) and further that, without an understanding of what is good, other important truths cannot be known. In this way Plato's thinking can be seen as a development of some of the ideas presented by the Pre-Socratics and also as a reaction to some of the relativist thinking of the sophists.

Background to Plato

Before we explore Plato's life we need to explore the life of another key individual.

As mentioned above, the sophists would charge wealthy men for the education of their sons. However, one of these wandering wise men was different. He did not charge for his services. His name was Socrates (469–399 BC). Unlike the other sophists, he believed that there existed universal moral ideals of, for example, justice and good, and that the truth of these transcended particular cities and their customs. However, Socrates did not claim to know what these truths were.

He gained great fame when a wealthy man consulted the oracle at Delphi with the question 'Who is the wisest man in the world?' and the answer came back 'Socrates'. Socrates himself professed surprise at this and said that if he was wise it was only because he, unlike others, realised how little he knew.

Socrates would confront the sophists he came across. He was intrigued, for many of these sophists claimed to be wise and he wondered if they truly were. He would usually begin by asking the sophists a particular question, such as 'What is knowledge?' or 'What is justice?' Having claimed to be a wise man, the sophist would feel obliged to proffer an answer. Socrates would then ask a series of questions until he had forced the supposed wise man to contradict himself, thus showing that he was not so wise after all.

What is of particular importance in all of this is the method that Socrates used. He was employing logic and reason whereas the sophists would usually resort to rhetoric, which they were experts in, or even on occasions to abuse. Many people see Socrates versus the sophists as the battle of logic and reason over rhetorical and emotional forms of argument.

Socrates was a controversial figure and not universally popular, particularly among the sophists. Like the sophists he had an entourage of young followers. In 399 BC Socrates was accused of *impiety* (not believing in the gods) and of corrupting the youth of Athens and was tried and sentenced to death by drinking hemlock. It is likely that, had he wished, he could have escaped to live in exile. However, he chose to remain in Athens, his city of birth, and willingly drank the hemlock that ended his life.

Was Socrates really guilty? Probably not. However, it is certainly true that he had built up a considerable following of young disciples and one of the youths who stood in danger of being corrupted by Socrates was a young man called Plato.

Plato

Plato would have been about 29 when Socrates died. Plato was born in Athens in around 430 BC into a relatively wealthy aristocratic family and it is thought he descended from ancient Athenian royalty. Plato lived during a period of war and considerable political strife. He would have been expected by his family to enter the political arena himself, but he became one of Socrates' pupils in his youth and this determined the path his life was to take. Through his own account we believe that he attended Socrates' trial, though not his execution. He was deeply angered at the treatment of Socrates by the people of Athens: an anger that is reflected in several pages of the *Republic*, where he is in search of the ideal city where such travesties would not occur.

After the death of Socrates, Plato travelled widely in Italy, Sicily, Egypt and Cyrene, pursuing his thirst for knowledge. He returned to Athens at the age of 40 and founded perhaps the first proper school in western society, known as the Academy. The school went on to last for nearly 1000 years. The great philosopher Aristotle was one of its first students.

To aid his teachings in his school, Plato wrote many dialogues, all concerned with philosophy. In many of the dialogues, Socrates is the main character and he usually engages in a debate about a philosophical issue with one of the various sophists. Indeed it is primarily through the writings of Plato that we know of the life and teachings of Socrates.

Plato's writings

There is some debate as to the intellectual relationship between Plato and Socrates. Socrates left no writings of his own, so most of what we know about his thinking comes via Plato's dialogues and this leads to the question of whether Plato simply recorded the words of Socrates, or whether Socrates was the mouthpiece for Plato.

We know that many of Plato's dialogues cannot be precise transcripts of real conversations, because often the historical individuals did not live in the same era, and so could not have met. Nonetheless, this does not show that the ideas expressed in them could not have derived from the historical Socrates. Plato did not record the date his dialogues were written; however, an analysis of Plato's writing style does give clues as to their chronology, and the agreed wisdom groups his dialogues into three bands classified as early, middle and late. The early dialogues are characterised by the fact that Socrates never proposes any answers himself; rather he is satisfied to undermine the beliefs of others. These dialogues see lots of short, sharp exchanges between the debaters. Typically we find the character of Socrates questioning a sophist on his knowledge of a moral quality such as courage, piety or friendship. Different definitions are put forward and Socrates proceeds by asking a series of questions to show that the definition is inadequate. He often does this by forcing the speaker to agree to other truths which show that the definition does not work, in other words by making the speaker himself highlight exceptions to it.

Book 1 of the *Republic* resembles the early dialogues in this respect and is believed to date from this period. In it Socrates demonstrates the inadequacies of certain conventional conceptions of justice as presented by various characters. He does this through a process of questioning and drawing out responses. When dealing with the sophist Thrasymachus, for example, the responses elicited ultimately expose the implicit view that he holds as to the nature of justice, and in so doing Socrates hopes to expose its incoherence. This stage leaves the characters in a state of puzzlement since their traditional opinions have been upset, but as yet they have nothing to replace them with. The sophist is forced to confront his ignorance, but as yet no positive knowledge is discovered.

These early dialogues probably resemble the words and ideas of the historical Socrates more closely than those of Plato's middle and later period. It seems likely that Socrates did not claim to know the answers to such questions, which is perhaps why these early dialogues end without resolution.

In the middle dialogues, it is believed we are seeing the true voice of Plato emerging, but still expressed through the mouthpiece of Socrates. These dialogues see Socrates' speeches become longer and longer, with fewer exchanges, as Socrates attempts to move the inquiry beyond this state of ignorance and toward true knowledge. The remainder of the *Republic* is believed to have been written in this period. Instead of ending with no definition of justice, Socrates goes on to provide a positive answer to the question. In this period of writing Plato puts forward a theory now known as the theory of ideas or Forms which is probably original to him.

Plato's later dialogues are characterised by some powerful criticisms of his own theory of Forms. In the *Parmenides*, it comes under severe attack, and the figure of Socrates is portrayed as having severe doubts as to its workability. In these latter dialogues Socrates plays a less significant role and is often a background part. This final period also produced a lengthy work called the *Laws*. Here Plato discusses the nature of political laws and outlines what laws a city state should adopt. This work contrasts interestingly with the *Republic*: where the *Republic* represents an 'idealised' or perfect city, the *Laws* represents a discussion of politics in relation to real or existing states.

This contrast echoes the shift in Plato's writing from his middle to late periods. Plato in his middle period is concerned with an idealised world – a timeless world of perfection – whereas the later Plato was concerned more with the practicalities of this existing world.

Plato's method – the dialectic

The method of question and answer used by Plato in his dialogues, and presumably practised by Socrates, has been termed 'the DIALECTIC'. Related to the term 'dialogue', the dialectic is a style of reasoning based on conversation (from the Greek *dialegesthai*, meaning to converse, a compound verb formed from the prefix *dia* 'with each other' and *legein* 'speak'). It involves Socrates in questioning his interlocutors in order to evaluate their claims to have knowledge of the true nature of ethical and aesthetic terms such as virtue, justice and beauty. In the *Meno*, for example, Socrates questions Meno's claim to know what 'virtue' is. Typically of his method, Socrates shows that Meno is unable to give a *definition* of virtue. While Meno might be able to point to individual virtuous acts, he is unable to say what virtue is *in itself*. Whatever definition Meno offers, Socrates is able to find a COUNTER-EXAMPLE. This shows, so Socrates claims, that Meno doesn't really know what virtue *is*. And if he does not know what virtue is, then Meno cannot truly claim to have any knowledge of which acts are right and which are wrong. Having recognised his ignorance, Meno is in a position to begin to search for the truth.

In outline the Socratic sceptical argument about moral and aesthetic knowledge runs as follows:

Premise: We cannot define 'virtue' (or 'justice', or 'beauty', etc.).
Intermediate conclusion: Therefore we do not know what 'virtue' (or 'justice', or 'beauty', etc.) is.
Main conclusion: Therefore we do not know which acts are virtuous (or just, or beautiful, etc.).

It is worth pausing here for a moment to evaluate Socrates' sceptical argument. What it assumes is that, if one knows what something is, one ought to be able to define it and that such knowledge is necessary for recognising examples of it. However, on the face of it there would appear to be examples of things which we are perfectly familiar with and able to recognise, but which we cannot readily define. Surely it would be true to say that you know what music is, you are able after all correctly to recognise and identify examples of it, and yet you might be hard pressed to provide a precise general definition of it. So it certainly seems we are able to recognise things without being able to define them. Despite this objection, we may still retain some sceptical concern that we are not correctly identifying something, for example virtuous acts, if we cannot define virtue.

Another aspect of the method is the famous 'Socratic irony'. Socrates admits to his own ignorance on the issues being discussed and typically professes admiration for the wisdom of the sophists and a desire to learn from them. He claims to want to question them in order that he too can acquire knowledge. However, as we have seen, what his questioning actually achieves is only to reveal the ignorance of the sophist. And anyone familiar with Socrates' approach will recognise the professed admiration for the wisdom of his interlocutors as ironic.

One way of exploring the method or ARGUMENTATION used by Socrates is to construct your own.

First, take a concept to be analysed and defined. For Plato these included beauty, wisdom, truth, love, knowledge, justice, courage and belief.

Below we have constructed a short example of a Socratic-style dialogue. Socrates' opening question often takes the form 'What is ...?':

Socrates   *Can anyone tell me what a pen is?*[3]
Generally someone with little philosophical know-how attempts to define terms by giving *examples* of, say, a courageous act, a just act, a belief, a type of love.

Mr Hayward   *This biro I'm holding in my hand is a pen.*
Socrates then gives a *counter-example*, circumstances under which that very same act/object is not courageous, just, loving, etc. The point is to show that giving examples of a concept is nothing like giving a definition.

Socrates   *Isn't it possible that the biro in your hand could be a sculpture, a mere imitation of a pen? And what of other kinds of pens, say fountain pens or felt-tips? Surely a pen isn't just a biro.*
The other characters, when they have been beaten at any

stage of the argument tend to end up agreeing with Socrates in a very grovelling manner.

Mr Hayward *Yes, Socrates, you are right.*
Another character then proposes a definition, based on common-sense prejudice, of the concept. This is better than simply giving examples, but because it is not based on any real analysis it is easy to show that it is incorrect/incomplete.

Mr Jones *It is easy to say what a pen is. It is something which emits ink.*
Socrates then goes on to show the inadequacy of this definition. He generally does so by asking a series of leading and distracting or seemingly irrelevant questions, to which his listener invariably agrees. Socrates' flattery puts the listener at his ease, making him more amenable to giving Socrates the replies he wants before Socrates springs the trap ('you have just contradicted what you originally said') at the end.

Socrates *So everything that emits ink is a pen?*

Mr Jones *Yes, that's right.*

Socrates *And do you know of the animal that lives at the depths of the sea that has eight legs?*

Mr Jones *You mean an octopus.*

Socrates *I do not know how I am going to win an argument against someone so clever, Mr Jones, but let me try! I don't suppose you know how an octopus defends herself, for only a marine biologist would know that?*

Mr Jones *I do know that, Socrates. It is by squirting ink into the face of the attacker.*

Socrates *Once again I am impressed. Now, would you say this ink was emitted?*

Mr Jones *Of course, for how else would you describe the escape of the liquid from her body?*

Socrates *Now, I'm sure you know the answer to my next question, unless you have had an accident and hurt your head.*

Mr Jones *I have not had an accident. So, what is your next question, for I am ready?*

Socrates *Is an octopus a pen?*

Mr Jones *Of course not.*

Socrates *But it does emit ink?*

Mr Jones *Yes.*

Socrates *So not everything that emits ink is a pen?*

Mr Jones *No.*

Socrates *Well, correct me if I'm wrong, but did you not say that everything that emits ink is a pen? And now you have just said the opposite.*

Mr Jones *You are right. Perhaps you could tell us what a pen is.*
Now the important part of a Socratic dialogue is the way Socrates invites everyone to suggest a definition, and then

shows each of them to be inadequate in some way. But each definition is a better version of each preceding definition, as the listeners learn from their mistakes. We may call this finding the criteria, or specifications, for the concept being debated.

Socrates	*I have no idea what a pen is.*
Mr Hayward	*Perhaps we could say that a pen is anything that emits ink which is not an octopus.*
Socrates	*Is there not a better definition we could give?*

experimenting with ideas

Try to construct your own Socratic dialogue. Choose an initial concept; it might be something abstract like happiness, perfection, friendship, duty or society, or something more concrete like a chair, a house or money. Start with Socrates asking one of your characters 'what is …?'

For a fuller version of the Socratic method in action, see the very loose rewriting of Book 1 of the *Republic* on pages 32–37 below.

The historical Socrates' use of the dialectical method to explore concepts appears to have been largely destructive. He seems to have been concerned to show that giving examples of, say, beautiful things, is not the same as giving a definition of beauty; and that those definitions his fellow debaters were able to offer were, for one reason or another, inadequate or incoherent. Socrates didn't claim to have knowledge of these subjects either; rather his point was to show that those of us who think we have knowledge haven't thought hard enough about the issues, and to get us to recognise our ignorance. So the method in the hands of Socrates examines and rejects existing definitions and ideas but does not generate any positive or new doctrines.

This must have caused many people to get frustrated with Socrates. Remember that Athens was undergoing a period of moral crisis. Society was genuinely debating the meaning of key moral concepts. In the middle of this Socrates was travelling around showing that all possible answers to such questions, be they traditional conservative answers or newer radical ones, were riddled with flaws. Such behaviour was always likely to land Socrates in trouble and doubtless lay behind the charges brought against him.

Plato in his earlier dialogues also seems content to end the investigation without resolving the question at hand. However his middle dialogues attempt to give answers. And it is clear from the *Republic* and elsewhere that he didn't regard the dialectical method as purely negative, instead seeing it as the route to true knowledge. So how can continual critique of ideas lead to positive knowledge?

To see how this might work imagine a fictional dialogue addressing the question 'what is beauty?' First someone puts forward a definition: beauty is objective and lies in symmetry. This we may call the THESIS. Socrates, through questioning, forces the speaker to concede that there are examples of non-symmetrical objects that are beautiful, the song of the lark perhaps. Someone else then puts forward a different, almost opposite, thesis, for instance that beauty is in the eye of the beholder. This new suggestion we may call the ANTITHESIS. Once again Socrates shows the inadequacies of the new thesis, perhaps by forcing his interlocutor to accept that there are some things that no one could find beautiful. Next a new thesis is put forward. This new thesis, however, merges what has not been rejected in the first two and so emerges from what has been learned in the critique so far. The new thesis may be termed the SYNTHESIS. This becomes the new thesis under discussion and the process of questioning begins again.

Now while this approach is destructive, in the sense that one idea after another is discussed then rejected, the process of critiquing definitions might gradually lead us closer to a genuine understanding of the concept under discussion. The process of exploring different theories in turn – the thesis, the antithesis then the synthesis – gets us closer to truth each time and gradually the process homes in on the truth.

■ **Figure 1.6**
Through applying the method of the dialectic, thinkers home in on the truth

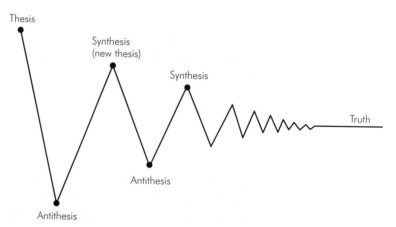

As an aside, this idea of the dialectical method leading to the truth was taken up by later philosophers, most notably Hegel and Marx. Hegel believed that the whole history of the development of human thought could be seen as a dialectical process with each school of thought being overthrown by its opposite. Hegel, in his masterpiece *The Phenomenology of Spirit*, attempts to trace this very development from the earliest pre-Socratic thinking up to the contemporary philosophers of his day. He suggests that we might view the whole of human intellectual history as a single mind arguing with itself, slowly refining its thinking as it heads towards the truth (which in this case was the very writings of Hegel himself!).

Marx took a slightly different approach. He thought that the key dialectic underlining society was not just one of ideas, as with Hegel, but one of material economic forces. Throughout history, and in various societies, there have been different relationships between the workers on the one hand and those who control the means of work on the other. History can be analysed as a sequence of changes in this dynamic, from slave-based societies to feudalism to capitalism. Eventually this shifting dynamic homes in on the true and final relationship, that of equal ownership in a communist state.

Politics in Athens

We have seen that the Greek world consisted of completely separate city states or *poleis* (singular: *polis*), each with its own laws and customs, united by a common language and ancestry. Each city state not only had its own government but also had its own way of governing. Many had kings or tyrants, others were ruled by a privileged elite or a council consisting of elders. Ancient Greece is also famous for employing the first examples of what is usually thought of as a modern form of government – DEMOCRACY.

Democracy, with a wide franchise, did not establish itself in Europe until the nineteenth century. It is odd to think that this form of government was in practice in ancient Greece over two thousand years earlier. That said, the democracy of ancient Athens was very different from the democracy of today. It's worth examining this difference a little further, as it was the Athenian democracy that formed the background against which Plato wrote the *Republic*.

The term 'democracy' is derived from ancient Greek *kratos*, meaning power or force, and *demos* meaning the people. There are, however, many different ways in which the 'people' could be said to have the 'power'. In the UK we currently practise a form of representative democracy. Individual citizens do not vote on the issues of the day directly. Instead, in groupings of approximately 70,000, individuals vote for a person who will act on their behalf in Parliament. In other words they vote for someone who will represent them. This group of representatives (known as Members of Parliament: MPs) then form a government and debate and vote on the issues of the day.

Individuals, aside from the occasional referendum, only get to vote in national elections every five years or so. In the UK, and the west as a whole, this form of representative democracy is largely thought of as a good thing. But how does it compare to the democracies of ancient Greece?

Athenian democracy

Athens is usually put forward as the first example of a working democracy in the world. Whether this is true or not is disputed. However, what is undisputed is that Athens was the most important early example of democracy. Athens had not always been a democracy; the form of government changed many times over the years. However, some version of democracy formed the basis of government in Athens from about 500 BC to 300 BC – encompassing the lives of both Socrates and Plato.

The democracy of ancient Athens was a form of direct democracy, which involved the citizens themselves voting on issues, rather than through any form of representation. Mass groupings, known as the Assembly, would meet at regular intervals (about once a month) to discuss new laws and also to act as the jury in trials and prosecutions. Meetings would usually involve 6,000 citizens. The population of Athens and the surrounding area was about 250,000 (including slaves). Only males over 30 were eligible to vote; these may have numbered around 50,000, and of these 6,000 were allowed into the Assembly to vote at any one time, usually on a first-come, first-served basis. So the great majority of the people of Athens, the non-citizens, had no say in government.

Six thousand is a lot of people to make a collective decision. The UK Parliament, when full, contains some 650 people and even this can be quite a noisy affair at times. Imagine this atmosphere times ten. Further imagine that, unlike Parliament, none of those present was university educated, and most had little understanding of the issues. With so many people present it would have been difficult to have had much calm and rational debate. The speeches made would have been direct attempts to sway voters one way or the other on matters that would be decided there and then without time for quiet reflection or thorough scrutiny of the evidence. Carefully constructed arguments drawing on reason and evidence would have been less effective than shorter emotive speeches. It is in this atmosphere that men who were trained in the art of rhetoric would have held sway. Those able to make powerful speeches, perhaps playing on people's hopes and fears, or harking back to the glory days, would have been able to influence the voters. The sophists, as outlined above, trained their young men especially for such occasions. Being able to speak well in public meant having power. Further, in ancient Athens, lawyers did not exist so if you were accused and placed on trial you would have to defend yourself. In such instances your life itself could depend on your ability to speak well in public.

Imagine if you will 6,000 men gathered on the side of a steep hill: farmers, sailors, builders, bakers, etc. The men would turn up on the day, usually with little idea of what was to be discussed and with no great understanding of the issues. They would hear the speeches and, with no time to go away and think, make up their minds there and then, decisions being taken by a show of hands. Many of the traditional ruling class thought that this democracy was little more than mob rule;[4] and indeed there are several recorded examples of how the crowd would get carried away with the emotion of the day. On one occasion it was believed that there had been mismanagement of some of the public funds. A group of ten treasurers were accused of corruption and sentenced to death by the crowd. Just before the last one was killed it was discovered that an error had been made in the figures and that the treasurers were in fact completely innocent – too late for all but one of them. This example shows that decisions made without sufficient time or expertise are often not good decisions.

Although the democracy did indeed place power in the hands of the people, the form of democracy practised in Athens was perhaps far from ideal. In particular it left room for corruption: individuals might well sell their vote to the highest bidder. It also allowed intimidation: with no secret ballot, there may have been occasions when people felt intimidated to vote one way rather than the other.

This democracy, ruled by the voice of rhetoric, formed the political arena against which Plato wrote the *Republic*. To some extend the Utopia presented in the *Republic* is a complete antithesis of Athenian democracy. Plato's state is an aristocracy, meaning rule by the best-born (from *ariston* meaning the best) or rule by a privileged class. Plato envisioned a state where decisions were calmly and rationally made in the interests of all by the wise few.

Plato's reaction against the democracy in Athens is perhaps understandable. On a personal level it was the democracy that tried Socrates and sentenced him to death. Moreover, Plato was himself an aristocrat and this is likely to have contributed to his distrust of handing power to the people. But on a broader level the democracy went against everything he had tried to achieve. One way of viewing the life and works of both Plato and Socrates is by seeing them as two generals in a war of reason against the forces of rhetoric. The sophists that Socrates would dispute with would often make emotional speeches appealing to the crowds using well-honed rhetorical techniques. Socrates on the other hand would be persistent in his use of reason – trying patiently to show the logical inconsistencies in the arguments of the sophists. Seen this way, the democracy of Athens was all about rhetoric, whereas both Socrates and Plato thought that governance should be all about reason. (Some critics of parliamentary debate would say that little has changed in two thousand years!)

An important contrast to the system of government in Athens was to be found in another famous *polis* of ancient Greece – Sparta. Sparta was a highly organised society run with precision and purpose. Boys would undertake extensive military training, living together in barracks until they were around 30. Girls would also receive state education that including military training. Essentially the entire citizenry of Sparta formed one big army. To sustain this, Sparta had an enormous slave population that would work the land and provide the means for the Spartan citizens to live. Kings and elder statesmen would propose laws which would be ratified by the citizens. The lifestyle of the Spartan citizens resembled the basic existence of soldiers at war: simple foods, minimum entertainment, early mornings devoted to developing physical fitness. Spartans certainly did not live the life of the privileged few, indeed the word 'spartan' is still used today to describe a basic, no-frills existence. This system of governance, although harsh, was also highly effective and Sparta became a military machine feared by many.

As suggested above, Plato's ideal state can be seen, in part, as a reaction to the rowdy democracy of Athens. But at the same time, with its highly structured and ordered society, it can also be seen as an envious glance in the direction of Sparta.

This chapter has provided a brief taster of the key background thinkers and events that influenced the thought of Plato. The influences range from the philosophical (Pythagoras, Heraclitus, Zeno and the sophists); to the political (the democracy in Athens, the regime in Sparta); to the personal (the influence and subsequent execution of his mentor Socrates). All of these factors are present in the *Republic*. This is not to say that the *Republic* is in any way derivative: far from it, it is frequently lauded for its originality. However, no book is written free from context, and a brief understanding of Plato's context only adds to the richness of the text.

Key points: Chapter 1

What you need to know about the **background to Greek philosophy and Plato**:

1 Plato was influenced by a range of Pre-Socratic philosophers including Pythagoras, Heraclitus and Zeno.

2 The concept of morality in ancient Greece was different from the concept today. In contemporary times we tend to judge individual actions as good or bad whereas the Greeks would use the term to describe people. Also when judging people the Greeks had to take into account the social background of the individual as the concept of good and bad was related to the function individuals were supposed to play in society. However the concept of morality was changing rapidly and Athens was in the midst of something of a moral crisis at the time of Plato's writings.

3 Plato's thought was shaped by his relationship with Socrates and can also be seen as a reaction to the philosophical approach of the sophists.

4 Socrates and Plato used a method of reasoning known as the dialectic. In the hands of Socrates this method was used largely to dismiss the views of others, however Plato believed that the method could also lead to the discovery of important truths.

5 The democracy of ancient Athens was very different in nature from the representational democracy in many western countries today.

An overview of Plato's *Republic*

Introduction

This book is primarily concerned with the middle section of the *Republic* (Book 5, 474c to Book 7, 521b) where Plato claims that, in an ideal society, philosophers should rule, and where he outlines his basis for making this claim, namely that only philosophers have genuine knowledge of what is good and so of how to govern. Chapter 3 onwards looks in some detail at these arguments.

However, in order to understand why Plato is addressing these issues, we need to see how they fit into the overall argument of the *Republic*. In this chapter we look at the structure of the *Republic*, drawing out the threads that run through the book, and the philosophical themes that Plato is concerned with. At the end of the chapter (on page 60) there is a flowchart which should help you further to navigate your way through the key ideas of the *Republic*, as well as a very short summary of the main arguments in each of the books.

We saw in the previous chapter that the opening book of the *Republic* has a form similar to Plato's early dialogues, with Socrates engaging in dramatic discussion with those around him, but without reaching firm conclusions. The remaining nine books are an exposition of Plato's theories, through the mouthpiece of Socrates, with very little substantive contribution from his fellow interlocutors. In the summary below you should bear in mind that, although we refer to the views of Socrates, it is Plato's own theories which are being put forward. This chapter contains the following main sections:

- Book 1
- Book 2
- Book 3
- Book 4
- Book 5 (449a–471c)
- Books 5 (471c–483e), 6 and 7
- Books 8 and 9
- Book 10
- An outline of Plato's *Republic*.

Book 1

The scene is set with Socrates engaging in a discussion with Cephalus, an elderly and prosperous Athenian, about the benefits of being wealthy. Among the rest of the group who will participate in the dialogue – the other 'interlocutors' – are Plato's brother Glaucon; Polemarchus, who is Cephalus' son; and Thrasymachus, who is a sophist. Cephalus suggests that money helps people to be more moral, or just. For Cephalus justice consists primarily in the performance of certain duties or actions such as making sacrifices to the gods, returning what is not yours and telling the truth. The richer you are the more able you are to carry out these actions, and so the more just you are.

Cephalus' belief that being just consists in carrying out a certain set of actions – in particular giving back what you've borrowed – is a fairly commonsensical belief. But Socrates is able to undermine this position quite swiftly by giving a simple counter-example: a case where it is not moral to return what you've borrowed. The example he gives is of borrowing a weapon from someone who goes mad and then asks for it back. Cephalus admits that in this case it would not be just to return it, since clearly the madman may do great harm with the weapon. The counter-example demonstrates that justice cannot simply be a matter of paying one's debts. Polemarchus' answer is based on the famous poet Simonides' idea that justice means giving everyone their due. This definition is an improvement over Cephalus' but Socrates is able nonetheless to find fault with it and the thrust of his objections go to show that it is not by the nature of particular types of action that justice is to be defined, but rather by the state of the person that performs them.

For Plato, Cephalus and Polemarchus represent typically complacent thinkers: people who think they know what a particular concept means (in this case justice) but who really haven't thought it through. It is down to Socrates to show us that we do not understand what we think we understand, and that we must work hard to arrive at a real account of these fundamental concepts.

The positions of Cephalus and Polemarchus, once undermined, lead readily into a radical scepticism about justice which is articulated by the cynical and aggressive character of Thrasymachus. Thrasymachus argues that justice consists simply in obeying the laws that a particular state happens to enact. To conform to laws is simply to bow to various sorts of social pressure. According to this view it is a mistake to believe that there is anything more to justice than obeying legal conventions. Thrasymachus' position, however, is not clearly consistent and he appears also to be articulating the claim that any sensible person should not conform to 'justice' as previously defined, since to do so is simply to allow oneself to be dominated. The strong individual should attempt to resist the pressures to conform in order ultimately to exploit others.

Justice or right is simply what is in the interest of the stronger party. (338c)

Socrates, through questioning, stings Thrasymachus into changing his definition to one that is more in tune with what he really thinks: that justice is doing what is in another's interest, injustice is doing what is in your own interest. Justice, on this cynical view, is a kind of pointless selflessness – a mug's game – and it is always better for us to be unjust.

Although he has exposed the tension within Thrasymachus' view, Socrates fails really to dismiss it convincingly. And at the end of Book 1 we are left in a fairly unsatisfactory position wondering whether Thrasymachus' proposal, that it is better to be unjust and immoral than just, might have something going for it.

To help give a flavour of Plato's writings, we have provided below a very liberal reinterpretation of Book 1 of the *Republic*. Please note that the purpose of including this is to explore the dialectic method used by Socrates and Plato, and that the reading of this text should in no way be seen as a substitute for reading the *Republic* itself.

experimenting with ideas

Go back to pages 20–24 above and remind yourself of some of Socrates' dialectical method: the use of questioning, his irony and his efforts to expose inconsistencies and so reveal our ignorance. Now read through the dialogue below and see if you can spot any of these tactics in action. Look out for the following:

1 Conclusions – when a character seems to have completed an argument (look out for words like 'therefore').
2 Leading or rhetorical questions – when a character asks a question to which he obviously knows the answer, but asks it anyway.
3 Analogies – when a character draws a comparison with something else or uses a concrete situation to make his point.
4 Contradictions – when a character has proposed, or assented to, a belief which contradicts another of his beliefs.

■ The characters
(In order of appearance)

Narrator	*The wise and friendly teacher*
Socrates	*The leading character, a skilful and charismatic debater*

Cephalus	*A rich businessman, in the twilight of his years*
Glaucon	*Plato's elder brother, a man of few words*
Polemarchus	*Cephalus' son, the voice of the common people*
Thrasymachus	*A cynical old man, skilled in the art of rhetoric*

PART I Socrates v. Cephalus

Narrator *Socrates and his friends are relaxing on the cool marble patio of Polemarchus' mansion – they've had a long and hard day at the festival. The vines fall rich with their bounty around the pillars. It's a Greek summer evening and there's nothing to do but talk. We catch them in mid-dialogue ...*

Socrates *You're looking very good these days, Cephalus. Tell us, what's your secret?*

Cephalus *Nice of you to say so, Socrates, you little charmer you. It's true, old age is treating me kindly.*

Socrates *There's plenty who'd put that down to the fact that you're one of the richest men in Athens. Not that I bear any grudges – at least you're not obsessed with money like some people I know.*

Cephalus *I've always said money is worth nothing without good character.*

Socrates *True, true ... Look Cephalus, I've always wanted to ask you, what's the best thing about being so rich?*

Cephalus *Actually, it's not what you'd expect. It's not the endless parties, the wine, the fact you can have anything you want. No, nothing like that. Because when you're facing the prospect of death you start to worry about other things.*

Glaucon *What on earth have you got to worry about? You're loaded.*

Cephalus *I have nothing on earth to worry about. People say that when we die we will be judged and the good will be rewarded and the bad punished. So I think to myself 'I'd better make sure I've been a good man, paid my debts, told the truth' and so on. Well, Socrates, do you know the price of sacrifices these days? Have you heard how much they're charging for entrails down at the Oracle? It's outrageous – 50 drachma for some scrawny chicken giblets! And another thing, the price of feta ...*

Socrates *Anyway, you were saying, because you are rich ...*

Cephalus *Oh yes, yes. Because of my modest fortune I can afford to pay my debts, both to the gods and to society. The way I see it is this: I'm a simple man, but so long as I've told the truth and given back what I owe in this life then I'll be seen as a just man in the next – and so escape punishment.*

Socrates *Hold on. I've always been interested in finding out what justice is, and you seem to have come up with an answer. Did you say that being just simply means giving back what you've borrowed and telling the truth?*

Cephalus *I did.*

Socrates *Hmm, let's think about this. So if I borrow your ceremonial chariot and refuse to give it back then that's unjust. Furthermore, if I gave it back to you and said I'd treated it*

	with great respect (whereas really I'd been using it to impress the youths in the market place), then my lie would also be unjust.
Cephalus	Two excellent examples, proving my point exactly.
Socrates	But what about this: suppose an acquaintance lent you an axe, and subsequently it is rumoured he has gone mad. Then one dark night he knocks at your door, foaming at the mouth, and asks for his axe back, muttering to himself 'Mad they said ... I'll show them ... Oh yes, I'll show them all right ... let's see if they laugh at me now ...' Are you saying it would be right to give him back his axe?
Cephalus	I may be old, Socrates, but I'm not senile yet. Of course that wouldn't be right.
Socrates	Even though you had in fact borrowed the axe from him and he was asking for it back?
Cephalus	No, I'd even lie to him if necessary. The only way we're ever going to stop these Mad Axe Murderers is to prevent them from getting hold of axes in the first place.
Socrates	So on the one hand you're claiming that returning what you borrow and telling the truth is the just and right thing to do. But on the other hand you're saying that sometimes refusing to return what you've borrowed and lying is the right thing to do. I don't like to point this out, Cephalus, but you've completely contradicted yourself.
Cephalus	Er ... Look, Socrates, I'm a bit distracted this evening, we drank a lot of wine at the festival, and my head's beginning to hurt.
Socrates	No need to apologise, my friend, I'm glad we cleared this up. I think we can conclude our little discussion by agreeing that telling the truth and returning what you've borrowed isn't the correct definition of justice.
Polemarchus	I disagree, and I can show you why you, Socrates, are mistaken and my father is indeed correct.
Cephalus	My son, I'm bored of all this talking. I'll let you two layabouts carry on the argument yourselves, you seem to have nothing better to do. I've got to go and see a man about a sacrifice.
Socrates	Some people just don't take philosophy seriously enough.
Glaucon	One day they'll learn.

■ PART II Socrates v. Polemarchus

Narrator	Glaucon's words turned out to be almost prophetic. For when Cephalus died the Athenian government confiscated his land and riches, and refused to give it to Polemarchus to whom it was due. But this is to stray from the story, and we must return to our friends and their noble quest for the truth.
Socrates	Polemarchus, as heir to this argument you must tell us what justice really is. Because we would all like to know.
Polemarchus	I think we can learn from the wise man Simonides [5] about this matter. He said:

> *The right thing to do*
> *is give everyone their due.*
> *So when money is in lieu*
> *pay your friend, 'ere you rue.*
> *Now that's all,*
> *Toodle-loo.*[6]

Socrates	*A moment, please (Socrates wipes away a fictional tear). I'm truly moved by such beauty. Obviously Simonides wrote some fine poems in his time, but judging by this one they weren't very philosophical. For if your great poet is right, Polemarchus, then surely the Mad Man is owed his axe and we should give it back to him.*
Polemarchus	*No, no, no. You're missing the point. 'Giving everyone their due' isn't just about possessions, it's about being good to your friends, and harming your enemies: in other words giving people their due.*
Socrates	*Ah, so that's what he meant. Couldn't he just have come out and said it in plain Greek? So justice means giving to people what we think is appropriate for them, whatever that is.*
Polemarchus	*Yes, and as I've just told you, that means helping our friends, the people we think are good, and harming our enemies, those we think are bad. Do you see what I'm getting at?*
Socrates	*Oh, you know how ignorant I am of these things, Polemarchus. I'm just asking a few innocent questions, keeping the conversation going, that sort of thing. But here's a thought – do you think that it could ever be just to actually harm our friends, or even, dare I say it, help our enemies?*
Polemarchus	*If I didn't know you better, I'd swear you were trying to irritate me by asking me such questions and pretending you didn't know how I was going to answer.*
Thrasymachus	*I'll tell you what, he's irritating me all right, that's for sure. One day, Socrates, you're going to get an almighty kicking – and that's something that's due, in fact ... it's overdue.*
Socrates	*Pray tell, Thrasymachus, you and whose army? But, I apologise, we must avoid such rhetoric. Our sophisticated friend here has given us an excellent example. So, Polemarchus, do you think that I should be given an 'almighty kicking' – would that be just?*
Polemarchus	*Not at all, because you are clearly a good man. And it can never be right to harm good men.*
Socrates	*Tell me, Polemarchus, do we ever mistake good men for bad and vice versa?*
Polemarchus	*Of course, we all make mistakes. But where is all this leading, Socrates?*
Socrates	*Well, my friend, correct me if I'm wrong, but didn't you say that justice means helping and harming those people we think are good and bad?*
Polemarchus	*Neither of us is deaf!*

Socrates	*And so by your reckoning sometimes it is right to help a bad man (because we think he's good), and it's also right to harm a good man (because we think he's bad). Yet I distinctly remember you also saying that it is never just to harm someone good. You seem to be contradicting yourself.[7] What would your poet say now?*
Polemarchus	*Doh! What a fool I've been, Socrates. I must have been mistaken about the definition.*
Socrates	*You know what? I think you were. Therefore it wasn't a wise man who said that justice means giving everyone their due. But the problem is we still don't know what justice is.*

■ PART III Socrates v. Thrasymachus

Narrator	*Polemarchus spoke with the voice of the common people, who believe it is just to harm those we think are bad. In a tragic and ironic twist of history Polemarchus himself fell victim to this distorted view of justice: he was executed by the Athenian government when it confiscated his father's lands. Cephalus' wealth couldn't provide much security after all.*
Thrasymachus	*I've had enough of this tripe you've been talking, Socrates. Just listen to yourself, you pathetic man. You babble on like a baby with all your polite questions: 'Oh pray, do tell me, Polemarchus, don't you agree that it isn't the case that Axe Men in chariots are people we think we believe are bad, but we really believe are good?' Utter rubbish! Why don't you just tell us what you think justice is or shut up?*
Socrates	*Don't be hard on us, Thrasymachus. We are ignorant folk, and clever chaps like you ought to feel sorry for us instead of getting irritated.*
Thrasymachus	*There you go again, Socrates. Playing to the gallery, getting everyone on your side, as if that will bring us nearer to the truth.*
Socrates	*You can see right through me, can't you?*
Thrasymachus	*Tell us all, my wise friend, what you think justice is. And don't say 'It's duty or advantage or profit'. I want a precise definition.*
Socrates	*Hah! You ask someone for a definition of '12' and add 'But don't tell me it's 2×6, or 3×4, or $7 + 5$.' How do you want me to answer – by lying? I'll tell you what, if you can tell me the right definition then I shall heap a thousand praises on you.*
Thrasymachus	*You know that I can't teach you without money up front.[8]*
Socrates	*I'll give it to you when I have the cash.*
Glaucon	*We'll pay for you, Socrates. Go on then, Thrasymachus, give us your answer.*
Thrasymachus	*Listen then. I say that justice is simply whatever is in the interests of those who have power. Anything that helps them keep their power is called 'Just', and there's nothing more to it than that. Now where's your praise?*
Socrates	*You'll have it when I understand what you're talking about. Are you saying that Glaucon here, because he has the biggest*

	muscles and is the most powerful, determines what justice is? I'm sure that eating lots of eggs keeps him powerful, but are you claiming that justice consists in egg-eating?
Thrasymachus	*Don't be tiresome, you're deliberately misunderstanding me. By 'power' I meant political power of course, in other words the rulers of state. So justice means obeying the laws of a state, and those laws are simply there to keep the rulers in power.*
Socrates	*I'm shocked. I thought justice meant doing the right thing.*
Thrasymachus	*You're so naïve, Socrates. Do you really think there is anything more to being just apart from doing what you're told? I say that you're actually better off ignoring the laws and morals of society and doing what you can to get what you want. If that means being unjust then so be it.*
Socrates	*Let's go back a bit. First, do you think rulers can ever make mistakes about what's in their interest?*
Thrasymachus	*Yes. After all, to err is human.*
Socrates	*In which case their laws aren't always just, as you've defined it, because the rulers may pass laws which are actually against their interest. Second, do you think that a law can ever be unjust – for example a law that banned sophists like you from speaking in public?*
Thrasymachus	*I'm rapidly losing interest, Socrates. Get on with your intellectual games.*
Socrates	*Well, if you agree to what I've just said then we can conclude that there's more to justice than 'whatever is in the interest of the rulers' and you, my dear Thrasymachus, are wrong.*
Thrasymachus	*Tell me, Socrates, do you have a nurse?*
Socrates	*What do you mean?*
Thrasymachus	*Well, she lets you go drivelling round without wiping your nose, and you can't even tell her the difference between a sheep and a shepherd.*
Narrator	*Some of these ancient jokes are lost in translation, but despite this the argument goes on long into the Mediterranean night …*

Book 2

We find ourselves at the beginning of Book 2, with Plato's two brothers, Glaucon and Adeimantus, restating the immoralist position that Thrasymachus has just put forward. Neither actually holds this position, so the purpose here is to give Socrates the opportunity to refute it and so prove that justice and right behaviour are indeed valuable. They want to know why we should be just, when it appears that we are much better off being unjust. It seems that Plato is not satisfied with the arguments Socrates has used to dismiss Thrasymachus and sees the need to build a more substantial case in favour of justice and why we should be just.

So how is justice to be valued? Glaucon identifies three kinds of goods or values (357b) that we might strive for. These different kinds of goods are:

1 goods that are desirable in themselves (intrinsic goods)
2 goods that are desirable both in themselves (intrinsically) and because of their desirable consequences (extrinsically)
3 goods that are desirable solely because of their desirable consequences (extrinsic goods).

This division between intrinsic and extrinsic goods corresponds roughly to a division in moral philosophy between DEONTOLOGICAL ETHICS (which says we are morally obliged to do certain things for their own sake) and CONSEQUENTIALIST ETHICS (which says we are morally obliged to do certain things for the sake of the consequences they bring about).[9] Most Athenians, Glaucon says, would say that it is only worth being just because of the consequences of doing so (358a). In other words being moral is a bit of a chore, but worth doing because we'll benefit, for example, from having a good reputation. However, Socrates believes that acting justly or doing the right thing should be put into the second category, that is to say that being just is desirable for both intrinsic and extrinsic reasons.

Read through the following list, and for each thing say whether it is
a) desirable in itself; b) desirable in itself *and* for its consequences; c) desirable only for its consequences.

1 Being healthy
2 Earning lots of money
3 Doing well in school
4 Falling in love
5 Being wise
6 Obeying the laws of the land
7 Being spun round and round on a fairground ride
8 Eating five portions of fruit and vegetables a day
9 Telling the truth
10 Doing philosophy.

Glaucon puts forward two popularly held reasons for supposing that justice goes against our natural inclination, and that people act in a just way solely because of the benefits it brings them. He proposes that people are naturally selfish, but if everyone pursued their own self-interest this would be damaging to us all. Therefore people agree to abide by laws that allow for mutual trust and cooperation. Justice, in the form of conformity to laws, brings benefits all round by stopping us from stealing, killing each other and so on.

In other words the origins of justice lie in a kind of social contract (358e).[10]

There is a second reason offered by Glaucon to support the claim that we are naturally unjust, but conform to moral and social rules because we have to live together with other people. This reason is presented in the form of a story: the myth of Gyges' ring (359d–360d). Gyges was a shepherd, a nobody, who one day found a magic ring in a cave in the ground. He discovered that the ring made him invisible whenever he wanted. He could do anything and go anywhere without ever being discovered. So Gyges, this ordinary shepherd, used the power of the ring to seduce the queen and murder the king and so become ruler himself. Glaucon concludes this story by asking us to imagine that both a just man and an unjust man had such magical rings. He argues that they would both behave in the same way as Gyges – in other words that underneath the veneer of moral behaviour we are all immoral and would do anything if we knew we would get away with it. Without any legal or social sanction for unjust behaviour it would not be in our interest to behave justly.

experimenting with ideas

In J.R.R. Tolkein's novel *The Lord of the Rings* there is a magical Ring of Power which had all the powers of Gyges' ring and more. Read this extract and then answer the questions below.

Boromir got up and walked about impatiently ... 'It is mad not to use [the Ring of Power], to use the power of the Enemy against him. The fearless, the ruthless, these alone will achieve victory ... The Ring would give me power of Command. How I would drive the hosts of Mordor, and all men would flock to my banner!' Boromir strode up and down, speaking ever more loudly ... his talk dwelt on walls and weapons, and the mustering of men; and he drew plans for great alliances and glorious victories to be; and [in his mind] he cast down Mordor, and became himself a mighty king, benevolent and wise.[11]

1 What is the worst thing you would do if you had such a ring?
2 Can you think of anything good you'd be inclined to do?
3 Do you think Glaucon is right, and that even a just person would behave unjustly given such circumstances?
4 What would happen if everyone had such a ring?

The picture that Glaucon paints of the value of justice is a depressing one: justice is simply something we conform to because we have to in order to live in a society – take away the threat of punishment and we would all be unjust. But Glaucon's picture gets darker when he adds that even in society the important thing isn't to actually *be* just, but simply to *appear* to be just. So being just without everyone knowing it is actually worthless, as can be seen from the example of the just man, who is innocent of a crime, but who is imprisoned, tortured and executed by the state. Glaucon wants Socrates to show him the value of justice even in this extreme case, i.e. to show him that justice is valuable for its own sake, irrespective of the consequences (358d). In other words, what Socrates needs to show is that it is better to be just and not appear so, than to appear just and not be so. Glaucon's brother Adeimantus adds that he also wants Socrates to show him that being just also brings benefits to the individual, irrespective of any (material) rewards it might bring (like power or money).

Prove to us, therefore, not only that justice is superior to injustice, but that ... irrespective of whether the gods or men know it ... one is good and the other evil because of its inherent effects on its possessor. (367e)

This, then, is the challenge laid down by Glaucon and Adeimantus. Socrates must now show why justice is good both in itself and for the natural benefits it brings to its possessor – conversely he must also show why being unjust is harmful and bad in itself. However, Socrates must first analyse what justice really is, for only then will we be able to judge its worth; this analysis takes up the next four books of the *Republic*.

Socrates begins his response to this challenge with an analogy: imagine you are asked to read some words in a small font that are far off in the distance, but you then discover the same words are written nearby and in a much larger font. Clearly you would read the large words first, so that you can then compare them to the small ones to see if they are the same (368d). Socrates then proposes that in the same way, in order to understand justice more clearly, we need to look at justice on a large scale. So rather than examine it in an individual person, he proposes looking at justice in the

■ **Figure 2.1** *Justice in the state is clearer to the observer than justice in the individual*

community at large. Having studied what justice is within society we will then be able to translate this understanding back to the individual to see why an individual should be just. So Socrates begins his investigation into what makes an ideal, and just, city state.

Socrates obviously is able to make this move because he assumes that justice in a city state is the same as justice in an individual. This may strike the modern reader as a peculiar assumption to make, but before we can get a proper understanding of his idea we need to wait until he has spelled out what he believes justice actually is in both. So, turning to his examination of society, Socrates argues that because it is hard for each of us to supply our own needs, it makes sense to band together with others in order to satisfy them. So the original social group would have served to provide the basic needs for food, shelter and clothing (369–376). And since it is far more efficient for each of us to specialise in one trade, and so provide one need for everyone, the simplest system will be if one person makes the shelters, another clothes, another food for the community as a whole. Indeed, because we all have different natural aptitudes, society will work best if each of us sticks to what we are best at and in this way the community as a whole can benefit from each of our skills (369b–370c). To follow your own personal inclinations, to say 'oh, I'd like a go at that' is to lessen the welfare of others and yourself, since the community as a whole does best when each member does their proper job. Julia Annas calls this division of labour 'the Principle of Specialisation'.[12]

The benefits of specialisation quickly fuel the development of this primitive community and as it engages in trade with its neighbours so the number of specialist roles expands as does the quantity of workers that it needs. Glaucon views even this expanded city as a 'city of pigs', in other words a very basic primitive society. What about the creature comforts that are brought by being one of the most advanced civilisations?

■ **Figure 2.2 The two classes of the Republic (the guardians and the producers)**

Guardians   Producers

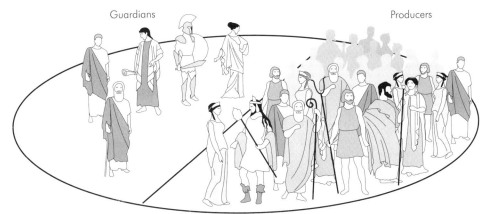

Socrates describes the kind of jobs necessary to provide the populace with luxuries, and significantly discovers that this more complex society is going to require a new class: those who will defend, police and rule the city, namely the guardians.

It is revealing that for Plato it does not matter greatly whether individuals actually want to fulfil the roles that society has assigned to them, or that they demonstrate a skill in. Plato says that people will be forced, for example, to be farmers even if they want to be shoemakers (374b). The common good overrides any individual liberty in such matters, and this attitude will become more evident when he describes the ideal and just state in Book 4.

At the end of Book 2 Socrates begins to describe the education that the guardians must have. For Socrates, the success of a state depends on the qualities of its rulers. So it is crucial to a state that it educates them well: offering them the appropriate curriculum at the right time in their lives in order to develop their character properly. Socrates compares the characters of the guardians to that of a watchdog: they must have strength of character, courage, persistence, intelligence and spirit. Yet they must also be fierce to their enemies, and gentle to their friends, which for Socrates entails that they must have knowledge, in order to make this distinction correctly. If the guardians have knowledge then the state is going to work well. This is the first hint of an issue that is to dominate the middle section of the *Republic*: the importance of genuine knowledge and of how to obtain it.

Book 3

Having sketched the basic structure of the state, Socrates goes on to fill in some of the details of how a state should educate the future guardians so that they might develop all the qualities necessary to be successful rulers.

Plato's ideas on education are radical. Fundamental to his approach is the insistence that the state must control every aspect of the education system, so as to leave nothing to chance. Thus the order in which subjects are learnt, the types of topics allowed to be taught in the classroom, and the qualities that must be nurtured in citizens, are all laid down by the state. Conformity, not autonomy, is the watchword in Plato's state. It is not important that young people in his state become independent free-thinkers (as liberal educationalists argue today), because Plato believes that a certain set of (true) values must be imposed upon the citizens. Those few citizens who eventually become guardians will see for themselves the truth of these values, and the goods they bring, but everyone else needs to be instructed to accept them. We might wish to question whether students who are initially taught to accept what they are told will eventually mature to develop the creative intellectual skills necessary to be guardians. Plato, though, clearly thought that this development was possible.

One of the biggest threats to the state, Socrates proposes, are the stories and myths that circulate within society and which the people are steeped in throughout their lives. Greek culture was dominated by the giants of Greek literature, Hesiod and Homer. Their epic poems reflected and informed the cosmological and religious thinking as well as the social mores of ancient Greece, and so held a powerful influence over attitudes and beliefs of the people. Unsurprisingly, Socrates sees this influence as potentially ruinous to his plan to control the thinking of the people and guarantee total allegiance to the state. Consequently he digresses to pursue an attack on certain types of art, music and poetry which must be kept out of the education system.

Socrates explains why art which is MIMETIC – i.e. which is imitative, particularly of human behaviour (392d) – can be so dangerous. Much ancient Greek poetry emphasised the more painful and problematic aspects of human existence; after all stories dealing with horrific deeds or terrible suffering, involving villains as well as morally upright heroes, are liable to be the more exciting for it. For example, Homer's *Iliad* graphically describes the brutal slaughter that took place in the Trojan War. Moreover, it fails to condemn much immoral behaviour, and its graphic details of death (of skulls being shattered and stomachs torn open) seem to glorify the violence, just as much as contemporary cinema is accused of doing today. Now, Plato regards such stories as extremely harmful: their moral ambiguity is confusing, and empathising with vicious people corrupts us. He argues that there is even a danger that we will become what we imitate (in Plato's day poetry was read aloud and the reader took on all the characters in the poem). For these reasons poetry and art would be carefully censored in Plato's state, and children would only be allowed to learn about art and poetry which avoids MIMESIS.

By the end of Book 3 Socrates feels that he now has all the ingredients needed to describe the ideal and just state. As we have seen, Socrates has argued that it is those who are best suited for ruling who should rule. The guardian class is divided into two: first the elder and better guardians, who are the rulers (412c); and second their auxiliaries, or soldiers, who perform the functions of the police, the military and the civil service and carry out the guardians' orders. The rest of the population, who produce and consume goods and services, make up the third class. Plato conceives of the state as an entity in its own right, not merely as a collection of individuals; and so it is the well-being of the whole state, rather than of any particular individual or class, which he seeks; and this is, of course, achieved by each class sticking to its function (420b–d).

Guardians

Producers

Auxiliaries

Rulers

■ **Figure 2.3** *The subdivision of the guardian class in the Republic into rulers and auxiliaries*

His sketch of this state, which he elaborates on in Book 4, is followed by one of the most controversial passages in the *Republic*, when he describes a myth that will be told to the populace in order that they 'buy-in' to this ideal state. This myth is in effect a piece of propaganda designed to ensure that people accept their lot, and work within their class to serve the whole community. The myth functions in the same way as the social conditioning that everyone receives in Aldous Huxley's novel *Brave New World*: as children sleep, they listen to propaganda that has been selected according to their class (Alpha, Beta, Gamma or Delta). Here is what Beta children listen to:

Alpha children wear grey. They work much harder than we do, because they're so frightfully clever. I'm awfully glad I'm a Beta, because I don't work so hard. And then we are much better than the Gammas and Deltas. Gammas are stupid ...[13]

Plato's piece of social propaganda is variously translated as the Noble Lie, or Magnificent Myth, and his idea is that it should be taught to all members of society as if it were true.

ACTIVITY Read the extract from the *Republic* (the Noble Lie, 415a–d) and then answer the questions below.

'We shall', I said, 'tell our citizens the following tale:

"*You are, all of you in this community, brothers. But when god fashioned you, he added gold in the composition of those of you who are qualified to be Rulers ... he put silver in the Auxiliaries, and iron and bronze in the farmers and other workers. Now since you are all of the same stock, though your children will commonly resemble their parents, occasionally a silver child will be born of golden parents, or a golden child of silver parents, and so on. Therefore the first and most important of god's commandments to the Rulers is that in the exercise of their function as Guardians their principal care must be to watch the mixture of metals in the characters of their children. If one of their own children has traces of bronze or iron in its make-up, they must harden their hearts, assign it its proper value, and degrade it to the ranks of the industrial and agricultural class where it properly belongs: similarly, if a child of this class is born with gold or silver in its nature, they will promote it appropriately to be a Guardian or Auxiliary. And this they must do because there is a prophecy that the State will be ruined when it has Guardians of silver or bronze.*" (415a–d)

1 What purpose do you think this myth will serve in Plato's ideal state?
2 Do you think people in ancient Greece would have believed this myth? Why? Why not?
3 Do you think it is ever justifiable for a government to systematically lie to its people? Explain why/why not.

So in Plato's ideal state there will be three distinct classes, each happily performing its own function. The Noble Lie ensures that no one dissents from their lot and everyone recognises the importance of sticking to their role, secure in the knowledge that this is in the best interests of all. There is no class struggle between rich and poor, and because the guardians will have no family ties or any material possessions of their own (see page 52), there is no risk of any conflict of interest amongst the rulers. Thus harmony between the classes and the unity of the state is ensured (422e).

Plato's ideal state may be a unified state, but it is also a paternalistic one, meaning that the rulers, who know what is best for the state, can make decisions on behalf of everyone else, occasionally without their full consent or knowledge. It also means the rulers can manipulate the populace, and broker falsehoods such as the Noble Lie, for the sake of the common good.

However, this ideal state is also entirely dependent on the guardians for its success. It has no constitution, no written laws, but instead relies on the wisdom and character of its rulers to make the best decisions. This means the education of the guardians must be exactly right, which is why Plato describes in such detail this education system. The rulers are chosen for their wisdom and love of the state, ability to rule, skill in good judgement. It does not occur to Plato (or at least he doesn't address any such concern in the *Republic*) that there could be abuse of the state if there is no constitution. For Plato, laws (as exemplified in fifth-century Athens) are trivial matters of administration; principles and ideals are to be found elsewhere.

Take the Republic as outlined so far.

1 Imagine you had to present a case for such a Republic to a group of Greek politicians interested in changing the way their society was structured. What benefits would it bring: how might it advantage the nation, or the individual?

2 Now imagine you had to present a case against such a Republic to Plato. What would you say to him, what problems can you foresee? How might it damage the nation or the individual?

Book 4

Socrates now moves back to the questions raised in Book 1, namely what is justice, and why should we be just? We saw in Book 2 that Socrates thought these questions would be easier to answer if they were examined on a large scale, i.e. in a city state. So the questions posed in Book 4 are: What is a just state? What benefits does it bring? And how can these answers be transferred to the individual?

Since Socrates has been discussing the ideal or perfect state, he reckons it must excel in moral qualities or virtues, and he names four such virtues – wisdom, courage, moderation and justice (427e). Rather than explore why an ideal state should have these specific virtues (we must suppose that contemporary Greeks would have regarded the idea as uncontroversial) he then moves directly to the question of what it is that makes the state wise, brave, moderate and just.

In answer to the first question a state is wise in so far as the wisest class are fulfilling their function, which is to rule. Wisdom, for Plato, is connected with skills of planning and good judgement (428b–d), and a state has the virtue of wisdom because it is ruled by the wise. The guardians are wise because of their education and because of their ability to reason beyond individual or class interests and so make decisions on behalf of the state as a whole.

And what makes a city brave? Again it is brave to the extent that the bravest citizens are fulfilling their function as auxiliaries. So a state is brave in so far as it is defended and policed by the brave. Bravery is defined as knowing what really to fear (429c) and being able to hold onto this knowledge under any circumstance or test. Doing a brave act is not enough, it must be done by someone with a certain kind of character: someone who is disposed to be brave (430).

So what is moderation, or temperance? Plato understands this virtue to consist in having self-discipline, being polite, avoiding excess and knowing what is appropriate. Moderation is different from the previous two virtues in that it arises from the relationship between all three classes. Moderation occurs in a state when a) there is total agreement amongst all classes about who should rule, and b) those ruled are deferent to the rulers. It is only because the rulers are wisest, and because everyone agrees that the rulers should rule, that a state can be described as moderate.

Finally Socrates turns to justice (432b–434d) and so we finally arrive at an answer to the question 'what is justice?' raised in Book 1, although it may not be the answer we were expecting. Like moderation, justice is about the relationship between the elements of the state. Socrates says that 'our quarry was lurking under our feet all the time' (433a); '[j]ustice is, in a certain sense, minding one's own business' (433b), in other words fulfilling your function and role in society. When everyone in the state pursues their allotted profession, internal conflict is avoided and the state excels in the virtue of justice. Plato clearly perceives a connection between the ordinary conception of justice explored in Book 1 – that it involves paying your debts, or each person receiving their due – and this revised conception. Doing what it is proper for us to do entails having what we deserve, he suggests, because getting your just deserts means getting what you need, and getting what you need is based on what you do (433e).

We have now seen what justice is in the state: it is when all three parts of the state are functioning properly and harmoniously according to their own job. Plato then reminds us that the reason we examined this ideal state was that we might see more clearly what justice is in the individual, or rather in the mind or soul (*psyche*). Now, given what you know about the just state, what does Plato have to find in the soul if he is to make the analogy of the just state at all plausible or relevant to the individual?

To understand Plato's analysis of the nature of the human mind, we need to begin with the recognition that our behaviour is the product of our desires or motivations. For example, I will eat because I am hungry, or punch someone because I am angry; or read because of a thirst for knowledge. All these actions are motivated by my desires, and normally I think of them as all coming from the same source, namely from my *self*; they are all, after all, *my* desires. However, Plato now asks how these different desires might be categorised and will argue that they do not all come from the same source. What he will try to show is that we can divide them into three basic types and therefore that the self or mind is not a unitary thing, but has distinct parts working together (or against each other) to motivate our actions. This basic psychological insight is found in more contemporary theories of the self, most notably in Freud who divided the mind first into conscious and unconscious desires, and later into the various desires of the ego, superego and the id.

Plato's argument to show that there must be different parts within the soul is based on the principle 'that one thing cannot act or be affected in opposite ways at the same time and in the same part of itself in relation to the same thing' (436b). Julia Annas calls this the Principle of Conflict,[14] meaning that if we have two conflicting desires then they cannot come from the same part of us. Plato gives an example of conflicting desires which he hopes will establish the divisibility of the soul. A person can have both a desire to drink alcohol and yet also a wish to control that desire; in this case he is accepting and rejecting the same thing at the same time (437d–439d). According to the Principle of Conflict these conflicting desires indicate that they must come from more than one source. It follows that there must be more than one part to the soul: a part that motivates someone to reach for the beer and a part that tells him it is time to go home. The conclusion is that our desire to drink comes from our appetite, while our control of that desire comes from our reason.

Plato goes into some detail here because he feels he needs to overcome our ordinary sense that the soul or self is a unitary and single thing. Nonetheless there are problems with his argument. For instance, the existence of conflict between desires does not necessarily show that they emanate from different parts of the soul. I may want to eat *this* death-by-chocolate-fudge ice cream and *that* hot chilli pizza *right now* but I can't eat both (although I have tried!) and the two urges can be said to be in conflict. So we would expect Plato, according to the Principle of Conflict, to say that they stem from different parts of the soul. But surely they come from the same basic source: my greedy appetite. On the other hand, we may complain that, if Plato's Principle of Conflict is right, we should have as many parts of the soul as we have conflicting urges. But this would very quickly get out of hand and we would certainly have many more parts to our souls than the three that Plato will identify. Plato might reply that this is to misunderstand the Principle of Conflict. Of course we can't eat this ice cream and that pizza now – just as we can't be in London and in New York at the same time. But this tells us only about the nature of these activities, and the size of my mouth, rather than about the desires themselves. The conflict in these cases is not a conflict at the source, i.e. at the level of motivation, only a practical conflict (that can be overcome given a suitable liquidiser and a straw). But Plato is interested in a conflict at source, at our motivations (e.g. to be greedy or to overcome our greed), and it is this conflict – between desire and reason – that indicates a distinction in the parts of the soul.

The first part of the soul is reason, that is to say, the part which thinks and reflects on matters when studying abstract subjects such as mathematics or philosophy or when considering more practical matters such as how to get somewhere, or how to make a cake. Later on Plato will show that reason is the part by which we come to know the truth and by which we apprehend the world of the Forms, but here he is more concerned with its role in governing our action. Reason is the sensible part that reins in our desires and so, for example, it prevents us from drinking lighter fluid or white spirits, even though we are thirsty. Its function is to rule the soul just as it should in the state.

The argument that reason should be in charge of the self is that it is the only part of the soul that is able to judge what is in the best interests of the individual as a whole; the other two parts only care for themselves.[15] Only by reasoning can we determine which desires we should satisfy and when, and if we simply pursue our baser desires without reflecting on the consequences, we will soon end up in trouble. The unbridled pursuit of pleasure is never a wise course to follow. With reason in control the individual is master of himself, rather than a slave to his passions. Moreover, such an individual is able to live a life in pursuit of knowledge; and the search for truth is, for Plato, the noblest calling of all. What Plato says of the soul applies, as we have seen, also to the state where it is reason that should govern in the interest of the community as a whole. This is why it is those who have reason in charge of their souls who should be running the state.

The second part of the soul is termed 'spirit' (in ancient Greek *thumos*) and is harder to define. This is the part that stirs one to action when angry or morally indignant, and is the key motivating force in the urge to do battle. It shares with reason the ability to override more basic desires and also, like reason, it can be moulded by education. But like our more basic desires it is a feeling or emotion, rather than a thought. The spirit overrides a desire if it is not a desire that is good for the whole person to pursue, or if it is felt to offend the moral ideals a person holds. The equivalent part of the state is the auxiliaries and, as in the state, the function of spirit is to police the soul. Those individuals with spirited souls will make the most effective auxiliaries.

The last part of the soul is the source of our most basic desires – our bodily appetites and instincts. The appetitive part encompasses an enormous variety of desires, all linked by the fact that there is some goal they all seek, such as food, drink or sex (580d–e). The examples Plato chooses throughout Book 4 emphasise the forceful nature of such desires, and the fact that they are unreasoned urges, blind to everything but their own gratification. The function of the appetites is to satisfy the basic needs of the soul that keep our bodies alive and thriving. Corresponding to the appetitive part of the soul, in the state we have the class of consumers and producers who are largely governed by the appetitive part of their souls.

ACTIVITY

1 Write down six things you have done today.
2 Now decide whether each fits into one of Plato's three categories: **a)** actions done from basic desire or appetite; **b)** actions done from anger or spirit; **c)** actions chosen through reason.

ACTIVITY

Read 442 in the *Republic* and complete the following statements.

1a) A state is wise when …
442c **1b)** A person is wise when …
2a) A state is brave when …
442b–c **2b)** A person is brave when …
3a) A state is moderate when …
442c–d **3b)** An individual is moderate when …

We have seen that Plato draws an analogy between the soul of a person and the state, and that the virtues displayed in an individual's character parallel those of the state. This means that a person is just in the same way that a city is: when each part is performing its function to the best of its ability. This means that reason rules, spirit ensures that reason has adequate motivational backing, and the appetites are reined in by the other two parts. An individual is just 'when he has bound these elements into a disciplined and harmonious whole and so become fully one instead of many' (443e). What this means is that the soul is a harmonious one without internal conflicts because the appetites have submitted to reason.

So we now have an answer to the question that began the dialogue of what justice is, both in the individual soul and in the state. But by the end of Book 4 Socrates is also in a position to answer Thrasymachus' question of *why* we should be just. Because a just soul is one that functions properly, he feels able to claim that a just individual is in good psychological health (444c–445b). It follows that living a just life is its own reward: being just means having a well-balanced and healthy soul, being a person at one with themselves.

We've seen that Plato draws a strict analogy between the soul and the state and argues that justice must be the same in both. It is in fact crucial that Plato maintains this strictly because (as we shall see below) his theory of Forms allows for only one true kind of justice in the world and so it must be the same wherever it manifests itself. However, the comparison doesn't seem to bear closer scrutiny. One difficulty is that the people who make up the different classes within the state are all fundamentally the same: they are all human beings, are all born of the earth according to the Noble Lie, whether they are workers, auxiliaries or guardians. However, things are not like this with the soul where Plato has argued that basic desires are very different from reasoned decisions as motives for action. Further, all the citizens are similar in respect of having souls with three elements, although they differ in how these elements are organised. This means that each class within the state is not exclusively rational, spirited or appetitive. The workers are not totally without reason, nor are the guardians totally without appetite and so within each class there are elements of the other two classes. But nothing equivalent holds for the individual soul for which each separate part is totally discrete.

Book 5 (449a–471c)

Book 5 takes a detour from the main question addressed in the *Republic* (what is justice?) by looking at the practicalities of justice in Plato's ideal state. It is possibly the most controversial section of the *Republic*: contentious in its day because of Plato's views on women (that they could be educated in the same way as men, and were equally capable of ruling, administrating and guarding the state); and controversial in recent times because of Plato's near-totalitarian conception of how the ideal state (the 'Republic') should be structured and governed.

When reading this section it is worth bearing in mind that Plato is describing an *ideal* state, rather than laying out a political manifesto for how he thinks Athens should be run for the next few years. Moreover, Plato's description is just a sketch; it does not give details of the ideal state – for example, Plato only touches on his assumption that slaves will still play a part in the Republic, he doesn't justify this or explain their role or status.

We know that there are two basic sorts of class in Plato's Republic: the guardians (subdivided into rulers and auxiliaries) and everyone else (the workers or producers). In Book 5 we find that this division is one of both power and lifestyle. The guardians have absolute power, whilst the producers have no power at all. On the other hand the guardians maintain a simple and sparse lifestyle to accompany their one passion – which is to rule rightly; whilst the producers have a rich and varied lifestyle, within which they are free to satisfy the full range of their desires.

One consistent and striking feature of Plato's Republic is that those with power, the guardians, are not rewarded with money or houses or fancy chariots or any of the other trappings that are these days associated with political power (463e–465d). For Plato it is essential that the guardians must not be distracted by worldly desires, and this even includes love of family and children. So the guardians are not brought up in families, and nor can they form and raise their own families. Instead they have a carefully arranged system of reproduction and childcare. There are festivals in which male and female guardians 'mate', and when the children are born they are taken away from their mothers and are brought up communally (460a–e). Plato believes that this will ensure that there are no family bonds, children won't know their parents, and parents won't know their children (457d).

ACTIVITY   In Aldous Huxley's novel *Brave New World* there is a similar contention that families and monogamous relationships damage the social good, and these practices have also been abolished in that ideal society.

Family, monogamy, romance. Everywhere exclusiveness, everywhere a focusing of interest, a narrow channelling of impulse and energy.[16]

Read through the following statements and for each one decide whether **a)** you agree completely with it, **b)** you agree partially with it, or **c)** you disagree with it. Write down an explanation for your answers.

1 Families (loving them, caring for them, fighting with them) are a distraction for anyone with a serious job to do.
2 Rulers would be better at ruling if they didn't have families.
3 Children who grow up without parents would make good rulers.
4 Property and possessions (owning them, being rewarded with them, selling them) are a distraction for rulers.
5 Rulers would be better at ruling if they didn't have any possessions.
6 Children who grow up without possessions would make good rulers.

The lifestyle of the producers may seem more attractive to us: they own all the material wealth of the Republic, are allowed to have partners and can bring up their own children. But this second class of citizens, the producers, are denied any say in how their lives are run. They are governed and managed completely by the guardians. They have no political power whatsoever, no vote, no local assemblies, no influence. The guardians rule over them completely, and Plato later describes them as enslaved to the rulers (590d). Moreover, there are no constitutional checks on the power of the guardians, no laws or rules that bind them, and they are free to determine the direction of the state as they alone see fit. So Plato's ideal state seems to be a kind of tyrannical one, with a ruling class and an oppressed class. However, as we shall see later, Plato does not consider his state to be a tyranny, for in a tyranny the tyrants do only what is best for them, whereas in the Republic the guardians do only what is best for the state. We shall see later that the rulers have grasped the truth about how best a state should be run, and that is why they are given so much power.

Plato's views on the position of women within the ideal state stem from his on-going analogy between guardians and guard dogs. This analogy is present throughout the *Republic*: for example, Plato says that the guardians must have speed and strength like a watch dog (375a); guardians must be able to make careful (philosophical) distinctions, just as a watch-dog distinguishes between friends and strangers (376a); Plato also talks about 'breeding' guardians from the best stock (459e), just as pedigree dogs are. So Plato begins his discussion of women in the state with the following exchange:

Socrates: Should female watchdogs perform the same guard-duties as male, and watch and hunt with them? Or should they stay at home on the grounds that the bearing and rearing of puppies incapacitates them from other duties? Glaucon: They should share all duties ... (451d)

Socrates then says that if male and female guard dogs should do the same tasks then they must be educated in the same way. Similarly, if men and women are to guard the state then they must be brought up and educated in the same way (451e). Plato's argument for the equal positioning of women in the ideal state is based on his claim that, although men and women might have different natures, these differences are not relevant to the kinds of jobs and functions that women can take on. So at 455e Plato acknowledges that there is a biological difference (women bear children, men don't). But for Plato this difference isn't enough to determine a woman's occupation; the only thing that matters when assessing who is suitable for which role in society is their capacity to fulfil that role, which is brought out during their education. Plato concludes:

It is natural for women to take part in all occupations as well as men. (455d)

To an Athenian citizen this must have been a very shocking claim: after all, women had no role in Athenian public life, they were not represented in the Assembly, they had no legal status and their views were not sought on public matters. But Plato is arguing that in the ideal state women will be able to rule the state alongside men – an idea which, in Europe at least, was two thousand years ahead of its time.

It is important to note, though, that Plato is not a feminist and he is not concerned with ending the suppression of women by men, or of drawing attention to their suffering or their lack of power. Nor is Plato a feminist in seeing men and women as equal: he simply doesn't, and consistently refers to men as being in general better than women (451e, 455c, 455d). Rather, Plato seems to be making a practical point that women are an under-used public resource, and in the ideal state they would be fully harnessed, working towards the common good just as men do.[17]

Books 5 (471c–483e), 6 and 7

The next two books of the *Republic* (plus the final part of Book 5) constitute a kind of metaphysical interlude. But they also contribute to the main argument about justice by showing why the wisest should rule the state, and why such a state would then be just. The three books also show why reason rules a just person's soul, because a just person will have knowledge of what is genuinely good.

These books explore in detail the nature of the rulers in the ideal state. Socrates is asked whether this state could in practice be realised (471c). He replies by distinguishing the ideal from approximations to it. The ideal is worth defining in order to establish a standard at which to aim even if it is impossible in practice to attain. Socrates now wants to identify the condition which would enable a state to approximate most closely to the ideal (473b). He answers that such a state will not be realised until philosophers become rulers or those we now call rulers become philosophers (473d). What therefore needs to be shown is that those who are naturally suited to philosophy are naturally suited to ruling and this is to be done by defining 'philosopher' (474b–c). The argument from here to the end of Book 5 is intended to demonstrate that it is *knowledge* that distinguishes the genuine philosopher and enables him or her to be truly just. True philosophers will be shown to have 'knowledge' while the so-called lover-of-sights-and-sounds has only opinion or belief (*doxa*). Thus the attempt to define the philosopher involves Plato in providing a sketch of his theory of knowledge and metaphysics.

Plato outlines his theory of what the world is really like: that this is the world of appearances and imitation, in which only mere belief and opinion are possible. It is only by coming to recognise the real world, the world of Forms, that genuine knowledge becomes possible. It is the guardian class, Plato calls them philosopher-kings, who make the intellectual journey to the world of Forms and thus attain knowledge. And it is because they have this knowledge, and in particular knowledge of the Form of the good, that they are ideally suited to rule the state.

These parts of the *Republic* are the main focus of this book, and are examined in detail in Chapters 3, 4 and 5. But, for a summary, see the flowchart on page 60.

Books 8 and 9

Socrates has already shown that justice is good in itself (i.e. is intrinsically good) because it consists in harmony and healthy functioning wherever it is found. But that is only one half of the challenge originally laid down by Glaucon and Adeimantus. He has also to show it brings benefits (i.e. extrinsic goods), and in Books 8 and 9 he attempts to do this. In Book 8 Socrates picks up the description he was about to give at 445e of the four different kinds of imperfect state and of the corresponding unhealthy souls of types of individual. The purpose of describing the four types of imperfect state is to show that justice pays by benefiting society.

The four types of imperfect state are TIMARCHY (or TIMOCRACY), OLIGARCHY, democracy and TYRANNY, and there are four corresponding individuals.

If you read 546b–c you will find some detailed mathematical formulas which Plato claims are necessary to ensure correct breeding. The point is that this world is not the world of Forms, it can never contain the perfect Good and Justice as the Forms do – it will always involve compromise and error. So, although the philosopher-kings are able to see what is right, when they come to actually rule they will make errors (546b). Degeneration occurs when the guardians are no longer doing their jobs, when they take a family and possessions, when there is no unity of common good but the rulers rule in their own interest. Such a state becomes what Plato calls a timocracy, because the rulers value *timê* (honour), and as a result are aggressive and exploitative (548c) – Plato cites Sparta and Crete as examples.

ACTIVITY

1 What do you think the corresponding timarchic individual would be like?
2 What part of the soul are they dominated by?
3 Will they be just?

Basically the timarchic state and humans do possess ideals of justice and temperance, and the value of reason, but they lack the self-discipline necessary to attain their ideals. They slip into glory seeking.

Two problems arise with Socrates' description of the imperfect state and the individual. First, the unjust state is not precisely analogous to the unjust individual: the timocratic state is degenerate because of the character and education of its rulers; the timocratic individual is degenerate because the spirited element rules. Basically injustice in the state is the result of the complex degeneration of individuals within it, injustice in the individual is simply one part getting out of control. The second problem is the one mentioned before: in an ideal state how do unjust individuals come about? There simply isn't the environment – and Plato's description of the upbringing of a timarchic son (549c–550b) certainly isn't the description of an ideal state.

The next stage on the road to ruin is oligarchy – rule by the rich (although it actually means 'rule by the few'). As people in the timocracy become more and more possessive, so they care less about justice and more about wealth – money, not goodness, becomes the measure of value. Rulers are those who are wealthy and possess property, not those who are wise. The problem with such a state is that each person, either rich or poor, cares only for him or herself. There is no longer any ideal of the common good, and poverty and crime flourish.

ACTIVITY

1 What is the corresponding oligarchic individual like?
2 What part of the soul are they dominated by?
3 Will they be just?

The problem is that Plato, in his obsession with making state and soul parallel, insists that the oligarch has 'a kind of dual personality' (554d), presumably to correspond with the conflict between rich and poor in the oligarchic state.

Oligarchy, Socrates insists, degenerates into one of the most hated forms of government – democracy. Socrates has already gone to some lengths (in Book 7) to show how democracies have no true leadership, persecute philosophers, and are at the mercy of the masses. Unity disappears in a democracy, there is no common good at all and there is no common government. Furthermore culture becomes PLURALIST, we can pick and choose as if at a style supermarket (557d). Just men cannot flourish in a pluralist society: Plato's ideal state maintains a strict control on education and culture to provide just the right environment for the creation of philosopher-kings. Some people imagine that Plato had Athens in mind, but actually this is not the case as it certainly did not promote equality, pluralism or freedom of thought – unorthodoxy was punishable by death and exile.

The son of the oligarch becomes a democrat, just as the son of the timarchic man becomes the oligarch. Each generation is corrupted by the previous, and the bad traits get worse. The democratic man has no principles or long-term plans; he 'spends, spends, spends' without thought for the future. Spontaneity is the key. Once again Plato is confused about the relationship between state and soul, and certainly a democratic state can exist without it being populated by people with democratic souls.

It is tyranny that Socrates singles out as being the most unjust. Socrates' account of tyranny fits uneasily into his account of unjust states. With democracy we seem to have hit rock bottom – how much worse could a state get? But Socrates has, since his argument first began with Thrasymachus, set up the tyrant as the bad guy, and now he struggles to show how tyranny is worse than democracy. It arises out of the power struggles that take place in a democracy. Its ruler, of course, is a tyrant. He has no thought for the city's welfare, merely his own. Everything in the city is valued in so far as it benefits him, and everyone in the city is a slave to his needs.

The *tyrannical* man, however, is different: he is not internally terrorised in some way – he is all too successful at attaining his goals, including ruling other men. Socrates, in his desire to show that state and soul are linked, has the tyrant ruled by lust (573a–575a). So the tyrannical character is a Freudian case study, obsessed with sex, but what has this to do with tyranny? Presumably Plato has tried to find a motivation that has no interest in the self, but only in its own gratification, and so 'getting what we want' does not entail 'getting what we really want'. All the tyrant wants to do is satisfy his basest desires. But this is not in his best interests; as such a person ends up with no friends, lacking trust, happiness or freedom from desire (576a). He is the most wretched of men (579c).

experimenting with ideas

Copy and complete the following table.

	Aristocracy	Timocracy	Oligarchy	Democracy	Tyranny
Who rules?					
How just?					
Corresponding character					
Corresponding metal					
How much unity?					

Plato proceeds to 'prove' that the just person is happiest. His proofs are these:

a) (581–583) The philosopher (the just man) will have experienced all three kinds of pleasure – the pleasure of each part of the soul – and can judge that his philosophical pleasure is the best. The problem is that we lack criteria (publicly verifiable standards) by which to judge pleasure. In the ideal state everyone may claim that they are the happiest, so how are we to know who is right?

b) Only the philosopher's pleasures are real. Other pleasures are dependent on the cessation of pain for their existence. Contemplative pleasures fill us more than corporeal pleasures – they are truly replenishing (585b–586c) and bodily pleasures have no value (look at 586b). Just people are 729 times happier than tyrants (look at 587c) because it is in them alone that reason rules.

Socrates, in the rest of Book 9, rounds off the *Republic*'s main argument. In Book 2 Glaucon said 'show me justice is good in itself and for its consequences'. In Book 4 Socrates showed justice to be desirable in itself, as health is desirable. In Book 8 we saw how other unjust types of life and state were undesirable. Now in Book 9 Socrates claims to have shown that justice brings good consequences – because it brings all the pleasures and happiness that being a philosopher brings. Justice brings PSYCHIC HARMONY. The question is: 'is psychic harmony what we mean by happiness, or has Plato simply redefined happiness?' He has shown us how justice resides in ourselves, not in the world, and he is assuming that happiness is brought upon ourselves and is not caused by our environment. This concept of happiness is one that may seem strange – but is certainly one emphasised by new-age, non-materialistic religions. Of course in a just state this may be true – but if you possess psychic harmony, yet live in poverty, would you still be happy?

Justice then produces happiness not in the way that money or drugs or chocolate or television brings us happiness (this is how a utilitarian might think of happiness as units of pleasure) but in a much deeper self-sufficient, longer-lasting way: psychic harmony. This is the benefit of justice and if you disagree with the arguments showing justice is good in itself then it is likely you will also disagree with this. What Plato has highlighted, in his quite weak arguments of Book 9, is the concept of intrinsic pleasure – that something is worthwhile because it brings pleasure in itself. Pleasure is not something that follows an activity such as a just act – it is there within it, like reading a good book, watching an amazing film, doing philosophy.

Socrates ends on the idea that there is a strange image inside us all: a man, a lion and an incredible many-headed beast. We should let the man rule, for he has our best interests at heart. To praise injustice, as Thrasymachus and the like did, is to allow the beasties to take control. That is why we should be just.

■ **Figure 2.4**
The beasts inside us

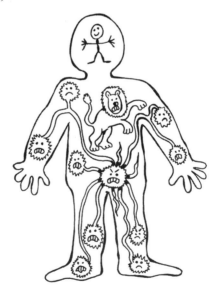

Book 10

The final book of the *Republic* sits uneasily with the rest of the text. By the end of Book 9 Socrates has answered the questions posed in Book 1, and has shown why justice is desirable both for its own sake and for the consequences it might bring. Book 10 is an awkward expansion of some of the tangential ideas in the *Republic*, and may best be seen as a kind of appendix or miscellany.

An outline of Plato's Republic

This flowchart shows the main themes – the shaded boxes indicate the focus of this book.

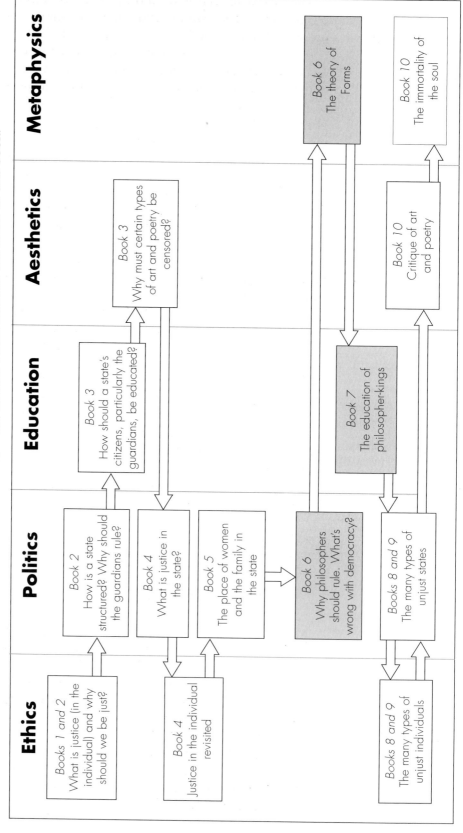

Ethics	Politics	Education	Aesthetics	Metaphysics
Books 1 and 2 — What is justice (in the individual) and why should we be just?	Book 2 — How is a state structured? Why should the guardians rule?	Book 3 — How should a state's citizens, particularly the guardians, be educated?	Book 3 — Why must certain types of art and poetry be censored?	
Book 4 — Justice in the individual revisited	Book 4 — What is justice in the state?			
	Book 5 — The place of women and the family in the state			
	Book 6 — Why philosophers should rule. What's wrong with democracy?	Book 7 — The education of philosopher-kings		Book 6 — The theory of Forms
Books 8 and 9 — The many types of unjust individuals	Books 8 and 9 — The many types of unjust states		Book 10 — Critique of art and poetry	Book 10 — The immortality of the soul

The first main section of Book 10 sees Socrates revive his attack on the arts, painting and poetry (which we first encountered in Book 3). The arguments put forward in Book 3 are that *some* forms of art and poetry are dangerous to the state, because they are imitative and can damage the soul. But the arguments put forward in Book 10 are that the arts are trivial and irrelevant, because they are *all* imitative (in the sense of mindless copying) and they appeal only to the lowest part of the soul. Yet following this dismissal of art in Book 10, we find a revival of Socrates' views in Book 3 that art is dangerous because it stokes up desires in the lowest part of the soul. It seems as if Plato held two inconsistent beliefs about art (that it is dangerous, and that it is harmless) both of which meant it was to be censored or banned in the ideal state.

The final section of Book 10 returns to some of the rewards that justice might bring, both in this life and in the next. Socrates first offers a fairly weak proof that the soul is immortal (608c–612a). He then goes on to say that just people are rewarded (by the gods) in this life, and that being just pays off in the end. Finally Socrates recounts a story of Er, a man who died and went to the underworld to witness what happened to just and unjust souls, and then returned to tell his tale. This myth seems to suggest that justice is desirable because of the rewards it brings in the afterlife – a claim that goes against the argument sustained throughout the *Republic*, that justice is desirable both in itself and because of its rewards.

Brief overview of the *Republic*

Instead of presenting a 'key points' section for this chapter, we have provided a brief summary of the main ideas of each book of the *Republic*.

1 Through most of Book 1 Socrates and the group discuss justice (*dikaiosun*): what it is and why it is worth having. Many answers are proposed, revolving around the sorts of actions that are just, but most are shot down by Socrates, and by the end of Book 1 the group has not reached a conclusion. The most dangerous proposal comes from Thrasymachus who suggests that justice is worthless and we should strive for injustice. Socrates is issued with a challenge right at the beginning of Book 2: to show why justice is better than injustice, or, in more modern terms, to say why we should be moral. The rest of the *Republic* consists of Socrates' attempt to answer this question. He initially does this by magnifying the problem of justice to a

political setting and considering the question, what is a just society?

2 So in Book 2 the discussion turns from ethics to politics and to how society should be structured. Socrates claims that within every state there are distinct roles for its citizens: basically those who make the rules (the guardians), those who enforce them (the auxiliaries) and those who work (everyone else). If this is the case then it is important that the education system is structured to ensure that citizens are capable of fulfilling their roles effectively. Books 2 and 3 examine this education system and how it helps to develop the character of the state's citizens in the appropriate ways. Socrates is clear that most poetry (which formed part of the traditional education of Greek citizens, and which carried the popular traditions, morals and histories of Greece) has no place in his curriculum.

3 In Book 4 Socrates returns to the question of justice, and argues that it consists in a kind of social harmony or balance between each section of society. A just state is achieved when each class (guardians, auxiliaries and workers) is performing the task for which it is naturally suited and avoids meddling in areas not proper to it. It is the guardians who are best placed to govern, since they will have the knowledge and training to do so. Socrates claims that just as a city can be divided into three classes, so a human soul can be divided into three elements: our reason, our spirit and our desires. And, just as in the state, justice in a person consists in harmony between these elements. So a person is just when each part is performing its own function and, as the guardians should rule the city state, so reason should rule the soul. So it turns out that being just isn't about the kinds of action that you perform, but the type of person you are. Justice in both the soul and the state involves having the best and most harmonious arrangement of elements and this is worth having for its own sake, just like health.

4 Book 5 takes us back to the details of the ideal or perfectly just state, and in particular examines the role of women and the family within it. Plato makes two radical proposals for his time: first that women have the same opportunity as men to be guardians, and second that families only distract people from their proper function and that therefore amongst guardians and auxiliaries families will be abolished.

5 The remainder of Book 5 turns our attention to metaphysical and epistemological concerns: in other words to Plato's theories about what the real world is like and how we can know it. His theory, that there is an ideal world of 'ideas' or 'Forms', which this world is a pale

imitation of, has become known as the theory of Forms. The argument in Book 5 is that genuine philosophers have knowledge of the world of Forms, and that is why they must rule. Philosophers, and philosophers alone, have genuine knowledge, and can guide the state justly.

6 In Book 6 Socrates uses two memorable similes (of the ship and the beast) to explain why philosophers are generally ignored by society, why this is a problem and why states which do not allow true philosophers to rule (especially democracies) end up in such trouble. Socrates goes on to explain in more detail why philosophers should rule: it is because they alone have knowledge of the Forms and in particular knowledge of the highest Form: the Form of the good. Once again Socrates employs similes to help us understand his position, the similes of the sun, the line and the cave.

7 Having established why philosophers must rule in a just state Plato turns his attention in Book 7 to how these 'philosopher-kings' might be chosen from the populace and then educated. The state controls the education system, and there is a prescribed curriculum that everyone must follow. Students who show aptitude go on to study mathematics and then dialectic (philosophy), until eventually those who have acquired true knowledge become the rulers.

8 In Book 8 Plato returns to the discussion of Book 4, namely that justice in the state and the individual consists in each element performing its proper function. In Books 8 and 9 Socrates describes the four ways in which a state (and an individual) might become unjust, because one element has moved beyond its function to take control. Each type of unjust society corresponds to a type of unjust individual, whose soul is imbalanced (the parts are not performing their proper function). Socrates' descriptions of the damage brought about by unjust societies (and unjust souls) gives us further reason to be just, so providing an answer to the question raised in Book 1. To this Socrates adds a final reason why we should be just, namely that it results in genuine pleasure and happiness (unlike other types of life).

9 Socrates' arguments about justice seem to be complete by the close of Book 9; however, in Book 10 he addresses a further collection of loosely related issues. They include: a development of his attack on poetry (which is more extreme than the criticisms outlined in Book 3); a proof of the immortality of the soul; an account of the rewards that a just person might gain in this life; and a description of the afterlife (in the Myth of Er) which is positively biblical in its account of the hell and suffering of those who are unjust.

Outline of key questions in Book 5, 474c to Book 7, 521b

The remainder of this book focuses on the best-known section of the *Republic*, from Book 5, 474c to Book 7, 521b, where Plato is particularly concerned with his exploration of the nature of genuine philosophers and the knowledge they seek in order to argue that it is they rather than the people who should govern his ideal state.

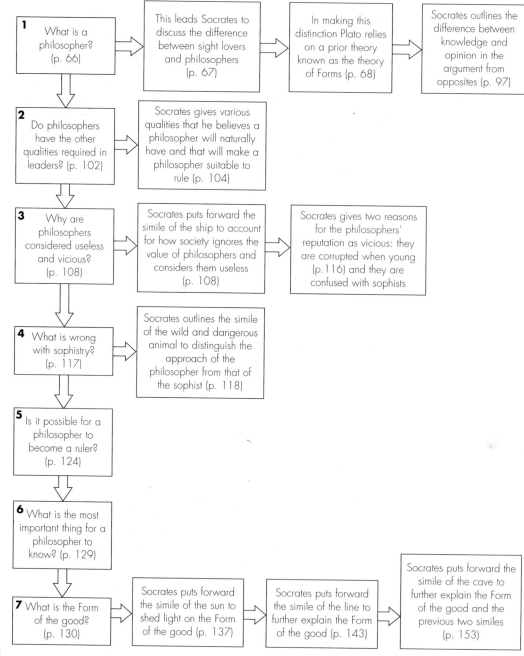

1 What is a philosopher? (p. 66)

This leads Socrates to discuss the difference between sight lovers and philosophers (p. 67)

In making this distinction Plato relies on a prior theory known as the theory of Forms (p. 68)

Socrates outlines the difference between knowledge and opinion in the argument from opposites (p. 97)

2 Do philosophers have the other qualities required in leaders? (p. 102)

Socrates gives various qualities that he believes a philosopher will naturally have and that will make a philosopher suitable to rule (p. 104)

3 Why are philosophers considered useless and vicious? (p. 108)

Socrates puts forward the simile of the ship to account for how society ignores the value of philosophers and considers them useless (p. 108)

Socrates gives two reasons for the philosophers' reputation as vicious: they are corrupted when young (p.116) and they are confused with sophists

4 What is wrong with sophistry? (p. 117)

Socrates outlines the simile of the wild and dangerous animal to distinguish the approach of the philosopher from that of the sophist (p. 118)

5 Is it possible for a philosopher to become a ruler? (p. 124)

6 What is the most important thing for a philosopher to know? (p. 129)

7 What is the Form of the good? (p. 130)

Socrates puts forward the simile of the sun to shed light on the Form of the good (p. 137)

Socrates puts forward the simile of the line to further explain the Form of the good (p. 143)

Socrates puts forward the simile of the cave to further explain the Form of the good and the previous two similes (p. 153)

Philosophers and sight lovers

Introduction

Having given an overview of the *Republic* we are now in a position to narrow our focus on the most philosophically interesting passages from Book 5, 474c to Book 7, 521b. The remaining chapters of this book focus exclusively on this section of the text. This chapter focuses on Plato's definition of a philosopher. However, in giving his account, Plato draws on a range of philosophical ideas that will not be obvious to the reader simply by looking at the text. To overcome this problem, this chapter starts by looking at the text but fairly quickly breaks away from the main theme to explore some of the background theory in more detail, before returning to the text.

This chapter contains the following main sections:

- Philosophers and sight lovers
  - The theory of Forms – extended analysis
  - Plato's theory of knowledge 1 – extended analysis
- The argument from opposites.

The extended analyses of Plato's theory of Forms and theory of knowledge are within the section 'Philosophers and sight lovers' as they are intended to help uncover some of the philosophical ideas contained in this important passage.

Philosophers and sight lovers

As we have seen, one of the key components of the political system described in the *Republic* is that every person should undertake the job to which they are best suited. This is of vital importance when it comes to the rulers since it is they who will safeguard the integrity and durability of the state by governing according to the dictates of reason. Plato reckons those who are naturally suited to this important task have to be those who are wise and who love the truth, namely the philosophers (473d). But in order to prove that it must indeed be philosophers whose proper function it is to govern, Plato needs to determine precisely what is meant by a 'philosopher', and for this reason he now turns to an analysis of what a genuine philosopher is.

We must define these philosophers who we dare to claim should be rulers. (474c)

The whole of the section we will be concerned with in the rest of this book is related to Plato's investigation of this question. The investigation leads him into a discussion of the distinction between the philosopher's knowledge, ignorance and mere belief, and so into Plato's theory of knowledge, or EPISTEMOLOGY. This topic, as we shall see, is also closely connected to his views about the ultimate nature of reality and of what kinds of thing exist in the world, in other words to his ONTOLOGY and METAPHYSICS. So in the remaining chapters we will be investigating some of the most fundamental and influential ideas in the whole of Plato's philosophy.

What is a philosopher?

It is necessary to bear in mind in what follows that, as the starting point of his search for a proper definition, Plato uses the literal meaning of 'philosopher', which in Greek means a lover-of-wisdom (*philos* meaning 'loving' and *sophia* 'wisdom'). So the true philosophers, in Plato's mind, will be those who can demonstrate a genuine love of wisdom and devote themselves to the search for truth and to a knowledge of what is good. Such individuals, as we shall see, stand in stark contrast to the sophists – such as Thrasymachus whom we met in Book 1, the 'salaried individuals' as Socrates dismissively calls them (493a) – who peddle conventional beliefs for money, and pander to the whims of the democratic crowd.

We will now focus on the argument from 474c–476d, where Socrates begins his investigation into the lover of wisdom.

Summary of the argument (474c–476d)

Read 474c–476d

- (474c–475c) To be a lover of something is to love the whole of it and not merely some aspect. Therefore the lover-of-wisdom (the philosopher) loves all wisdom or learning, that is *wisdom-as-such*, and not just wisdom of a certain kind.
- (475d–e) The genuine philosopher is a lover-of-truth. This means that he or she loves the *one thing* that is beauty, justice, etc. He or she is not simply a lover of a *multiplicity* of beautiful things, that is of 'sights and sounds'.
- (476a–b) Thus while the lover-of-sights loves sensible instances of beautiful things, the true philosopher loves 'real beauty': that is, the essential nature of beauty itself, or the 'Form' (*eidos*) of beauty.

Interpretation

Socrates is claiming that true philosophers are those who love the truth. But he goes on to say that this account is too simple as it would also include what he calls 'sight lovers', by which he means people who rush around willy-nilly in search of all manner of knowledge and experience. So, it seems that a lover of wisdom is too imprecise an expression since it could be applied to a number of very different types of person, such as train spotters, film buffs or pub-quiz fanatics. In order to distinguish these sight lovers from the true philosophers, Socrates goes on to suggest that justice, beauty, goodness, etc. are all single things, and that it is of these that true philosophers seek knowledge. By contrast the sight lovers love the many things that partake in or resemble, for example, beauty, such as particular flowers, pieces of music, poems or sunsets. What these lovers miss is the single thing – beauty itself – that lies behind the many beautiful things we see and hear around us.

An initial way of making sense of these claims is to imagine, as Plato does, two different types of person. Person A revels in experiencing various forms of art, music and so on. Person A wants to fill her mind with as many aesthetic experiences as possible. Person B, on the other hand, takes a very different approach. In addition to experiencing many different forms of art, she also wishes to construct a theory as to the true nature of art. Like A she enjoys seeing plays, and going to concerts, but also wants to theorise about the nature of drama, comedy and music. Person A simply enjoys the superficial experience, whereas B wants to penetrate deeper into it and discover its true nature. And the same difference of approach may be applied in other spheres of human experience. For example, A might also be interested in collecting many different types of butterfly; her experience over many years would provide her with a familiarity with the many different species and varieties that exist. B, on the other hand, might be more interested in conducting a scientific investigation into the life-cycle, feeding and breeding habits, the genetic make-up and so on of butterflies. This study would reveal what butterflies all have in common, what makes them the kind of creatures they are, and would provide a deeper understanding of butterflies.

Person A could be said to be a lover of wisdom, in that she tries to gain knowledge through experiencing as much of the world as possible. But B's more penetrating approach is more likely to develop a genuine understanding. What Plato is arguing is that we should reserve the term 'philosopher' for this second type of thinker. The true philosopher is not satisfied with a superficial collection of information through the senses; rather she searches for the explanation or rationale lying beneath the appearances.

In these passages Plato is drawing on a theoretical framework that owes much to Pythagoras' two-worlds view discussed in Chapter 1, although it is not explicitly articulated. Socrates and the other characters in the dialogue are familiar with the basic assumptions and language of this way of thinking, and Glaucon, once reminded (474dff.), is happy to allow the argument to progress relatively swiftly and with little need for Socrates to defend or explain the moves he makes. However, in order for us properly to make sense of the argument it will be necessary here to pause while we flesh out the basic tenets of the theory which underlies the discussion, a theory which has come to be known as Plato's 'theory of ideas' or 'Forms'.

The theory of Forms – extended analysis

The exact nature of Plato's theory of Forms is widely disputed. This is in part because nowhere in his writings does Plato give a straightforward account of it. Presumably the theory and the arguments for it would have been given in some detail and taught at the Academy, and so by the time it reached the dialogues a familiarity could be assumed. As a result, scholars have to try to piece together the theory from the references to it here and there in various dialogues.

Despite this the fundamentals of the theory of Forms are pretty clear. At heart it can be viewed as an attempt to explain the relationship between particular things, on the one hand, and what philosophers call UNIVERSALS on the other. Take as an example of a particular thing the red rose in the vase on my desk. This is a specific individual object existing in a certain moment of time and in a specific position in space. But notice that this rose has various things in common with other particular things in the world. Its redness is not peculiar to it, but is a feature shared by many things. Similarly it is not the only rose in the world; there have been, are and will be many other roses. Now, what is it that all individual red things have in common? What is it that all roses share? To put the question another way, since the general terms 'red' or 'rose' don't simply refer to specific occurrences of red things and of roses, what do they refer to? The answer is 'universals'. Universals are what particular things have in common and that to which general terms refer.

Now, some philosophers, such as Plato's student Aristotle, hold that universals don't exist over and above the individual things which instantiate them. So we cannot separate redness itself from the many examples of red things in the world, and the word 'rose' doesn't refer to anything other than all the many individual roses. Plato, by contrast, held that general terms refer to independently existing entities. The universal 'red' is a real but non-physical thing existing outside of space and time. These universals aren't objects you can observe with your senses, rather they exist in a 'supersensible' realm comprehensible only by the mind. These entities are known as Platonic 'ideas' (*eidos*) or 'Forms', hence Plato's 'theory of Forms'.

Forms are, for Plato, akin to perfect versions of the particulars that exist in the physical world. Thus, the Form of the rose is an ideal rose and all the individual roses – like the one on my desk – are imperfect copies of the ideal. This way of understanding the relationship of particulars to universals is perhaps best understood if we approach the issue through mathematical or geometric concepts, such as those of a circle or straight line. No line ever drawn by humans will ever be absolutely straight. If we examine any line closely enough, through a microscope perhaps, there will inevitably be flaws and wobbles. And yet we all have a perfectly good idea of what a straight line should be. Indeed, it is only because we have such an idea that we can tell when and how any individual line falls short of being perfect. What this observation suggested to Plato was that our idea of 'straight line' does not come from observation of any particular lines that we have encountered in the physical world, rather what we are contemplating when we think of a straight line is something purely mental; something we recognise by the mind alone.

So the 'Form' of a straight line is an ideal by which we gauge and adjudge all attempted drawings of it. It is grasped with our mind not our eyes, although we may initially use our eyes to put ourselves on the right track. And while there are many attempted 'straight' lines in the world – just grasp a ruler and a pencil and you can add to the number – none of these is ever perfect. However, the Form is a singular entity, which is perfect, unchanging and the same for everyone.

Another important example for Plato is numbers. When teaching a child numbers we may point out many examples of pairs of objects and repeat the word 'two'. Initially the child may simply echo back the word to gain approval but eventually a moment will come when the child grasps the concept of 'two-ness'. In Plato's terms we might say that the child has grasped the Form of 'two'. This Form is not something that you can see or touch. The number two itself is not something that might appear in space and time like a physical thing. Rather, it is something that the mind grasps, and unlike everything in the physical world which must eventually decay and die, is eternal and unchanging. It is the same Form which has been and continues to be grasped by children throughout the world, for the concept is universal. Moreover, the recognition of the Form is what enables the child to understand a key aspect of the world. The understanding of a simple piece of arithmetic, say that two added to two makes four, enables us to know that, whenever two objects are added to two more, four objects will result. Thus knowledge that is grasped by the mind of an eternal and universal truth concerned with the realm of Forms has straightforward application to the physical world perceived by the senses. Plato thought that the same applies for all true knowledge. In other words knowledge should involve the mind grasping the singular Forms that underpin and explain the many 'sights and sounds' appearing to the senses.

As a final example let's consider another non-mathematical concept, such as beauty, which Plato believed operates in much the same way. A particular painting may be beautiful, as may be a sunset or even a horse, but what do all these things have in common? Presumably 'beauty' itself. But clearly beauty as such does not exist in the physical world. All that we can ever see around us are examples of beautiful things, in the same way that the number two does not exist, only pairs of objects. 'Beauty' is a concept, an ideal by which we judge the relative beauty of objects in the world. To fully understand beauty would thus be to grasp the Form of it, in the same way as fully understanding 'two-ness' or a straight line is to grasp a timeless concept that can then be applied to all cases in the world.

Plato uses a variety of similes to describe the relation that obtains between particulars and the Forms. Sometimes he speaks of the Form being 'present' in an object, or of the object 'participating in' (*metechein* 476d) the Form. Alternatively he speaks of the object as an 'approximation', 'copy' or 'imitation' of the Form (475e–476d). These similes allow for particulars to admit of degrees of approximation to Forms. The Form may also be thought of as akin to a mould or blueprint determining what a set of particulars of a certain kind have in common, while no two particulars need ever be identical. It is our recognition of the Form in the particular which enables us to see that it belongs to a certain class of thing.

Later in the *Republic* Plato contrasts Forms and sensible objects by saying the former are 'forever', or 'always are' whereas the latter 'wander in generation and decay'. The Forms are said to inhabit 'the realm unaffected by the vicissitudes of change and decay' (485b). As we have seen, this means that while any particular is subject to temporal

[handwritten margin note: beauty is not real.]

qualifications and in the course of things is subject to change, the Form, like the number three, or the perfect circle, is eternal and unalterable.

Now, Plato's theory has much in it that is fairly uncontroversial, for it is clear that our understanding of the world must involve the apprehension of universals and these universals are not physical things. However, what is more controversial is that, according to the standard interpretation, he allies this insight to the metaphysical claim that the Forms have real existence independently of human minds. The Forms occupy their own realm outside of space and time: an eternal world which it is the privilege of our intellect to be able to apprehend. And because Forms are perfect, unchanging and universal they actually possess a higher degree of reality than the world of physical objects which we apprehend with the senses.

■ **Figure 3.1**

a) Ordinary picture of concepts
Two people grasp the concept of a straight line in their own minds: the concept does not 'exist' outside their minds

b) Plato's picture of concepts/Forms
Two people grasp the same concept of a straight line, a concept that has an existence independent of their minds

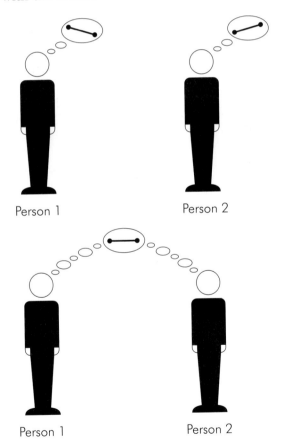

Person 1   Person 2

Person 1   Person 2

This metaphysical dimension to Plato's theory also becomes associated with his views on life after death and the nature of the human soul. In various other dialogues, Plato argues that the soul is immaterial and immortal (e.g. *Phaedo, Meno*) and that before our physical birth it inhabited the realm of the Forms, where it was able directly to apprehend the true

Forms of beauty, justice, triangle, two, rose, and so on. When we are born into this world, the trauma of the process leads us to forget our previous existence, but the knowledge of the Forms remains deep within us. In this life we may strive to recover the knowledge we innately possess, and all learning is in reality a recollection of ideas buried deep within the mind. The role of reason and philosophy is to make explicit the knowledge within us.

Plato's model of knowledge generally is figured by the nature of mathematics. In maths and geometry a singular truth can be applied to many examples in the physical world: for example, the same geometric principle can be used to map out a plan for any number of houses. Moreover, as we have seen, the truths of maths and geometry are grasped by the mind rather than the senses: they are certain, timeless and universal. By treating other areas of human enquiry, such as aesthetics or ethics, on the model of mathematics, Plato hoped to be able to discover eternal and universal truths concerning the nature of beauty and justice for example. Whether or not knowledge in these areas can be treated like knowledge in mathematics is another matter.

In summary, the central claim of Plato's epistemology (or theory of knowledge) is that true knowledge consists not of information gained from the senses, but in grasping the Forms. And this view of knowledge involves a commitment to a certain ontology (or theory of being), namely that there exist two worlds: the physical world revealed to the senses and an intelligible world revealed by the mind (see Figure 3.2).

As mentioned above, the exact nature of Plato's theory of Forms is disputed. The account given so far can loosely be termed the standard interpretation. One of the key features of this interpretation is the idea that Plato believed that the Forms actually exist independently of human thoughts. In philosophical language, this interpretation claims that Plato is making an ontological commitment to the existence of Forms. This idea might seem a little strange. After all, what sort of existence could a Form have? The Form of beauty cannot itself be a beautiful object; somehow it encompasses the idea of all beauty, but does not actually exist as a physical object. What would it be like to apprehend such a Form? The idea of concepts somehow existing is not easy to understand; after all it's hard to imagine bumping into the number 7 when walking down the high street. For some commentators the idea is so odd that they claim that Plato could not actually have believed it. They claim that Plato did not really believe the Forms existed separately from the human mind. And that any talk of the Forms as distinct entities is just use of metaphorical language (something that Plato is very keen on!).

The world of Forms is perceived by the mind. This is sometimes called the intelligible realm

World 1

World 2

The sensible world is filled with objects that are perceived by the senses

■ Figure 3.2
Plato's two-world view

More on this 'secular' interpretation of Plato's theory of Forms can be found on page 141.

■ Understanding the context of Plato's theory of Forms

Although this is an original theory, we can clearly see the influence of pre-Socratic thought in Plato's ideas. From Pythagoras we see the idea of a separate reality that somehow underlies the world we live in, and one that is apprehended through reason. From Heraclitus we see a world of perception that is constantly changing and from which knowledge cannot be gained. From Zeno we see a static world (the world of Forms) that is unchanging and that can be apprehended through reason.

Plato's theory may seem to be quite radical – that there exists a separate world of Forms, consisting of beauty, good, etc. and of perfect objects. From an ontological perspective (i.e. a theory about what exists in the universe) Plato's theory is not widely believed today (if it is at all), although it has many features in common with other widely held beliefs. From an epistemological perspective (a theory about how we gain knowledge), Plato's theory is not dissimilar to many other widely held beliefs.

As we saw above with the philosophy of Zeno, in its structure, Plato's theory of Forms is making claims that are similar to many of the world's religions. There is the claim that there are two distinct realms of existence, a claim preached by most religions with concepts of heaven/afterlife. There is the claim that the world we live in is somehow a less perfect version of the other world, again a claim shared by most religions. There is the view that the other, more perfect world is eternal and unchanging, once more a view that resonates with most conceptions of heaven. There is the claim that true knowledge must somehow come from the other, more perfect world; a claim endorsed by most religions which see true knowledge as deriving from scriptures or other forms of divine revelation.

It would seem that the basic structures of Plato's theory of Forms are not that strange at all, indeed the theory seems to be similar to many beliefs held in many different cultures. What distinguished Plato's theory is that, prima facie, it is not a religious theory at all; it is a philosophical account of what the world is like and how knowledge can be gained.

The Forms answering relativism

As well as reflecting some of the ideas of the Pre-Socratic philosophers, Plato's theory can also be seen as a reaction to some of the relativist thinking prevalent at the time, as preached by some of the sophists. Relativists claim there are no objective moral truths; moral beliefs are a matter of subjective opinion. Although Socrates probably believed that there was a moral truth, his constant questioning, arguing and undermining of any attempt to answer moral questions probably served to enhance the feeling that moral truth was impossible.

Plato's theory of Forms, however, suggests that morality and also aesthetics somehow exist independently of human thought. In claiming this, Plato's theory provides an answer to the sceptics.

According to a common theory of truth, a sentence or proposition (i.e. a sentence that asserts something about the world) is true when the proposition corresponds to a fact in the world.

In Figure 3.3 the proposition asserts that behind the wall there are three pigs. In this case the proposition corresponds to a fact (behind the wall there are indeed three pigs), so the proposition is true. If there were no pigs, or four pigs, then the proposition would not correspond to the fact and the sentence would not be true.

■ Figure 3.3
***The correspondence
theory of truth***

*The proposition
corresponds to the fact so
the proposition is true*

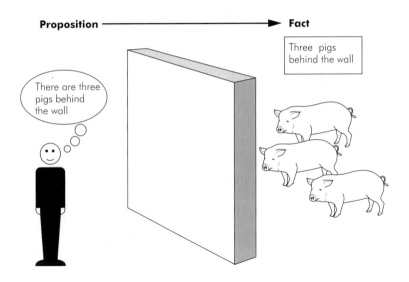

This is all well and good when dealing with pigs and walls.
However, the situation becomes less obvious when talking
about moral beliefs. The relativists would claim that, in regard
to moral propositions, there are no moral facts in the world
(or beyond) to which moral propositions could correspond.
This means that moral propositions cannot really be said to be
true.

■ Figure 3.4
***What could the
proposition
correspond to in
order for it to be
true or false?***

Here the onlooker makes the proposition that it is wrong to
shoot the fox. However, in this case it is not clear what fact
this proposition could correspond to. You could claim that the
'fact' is that the majority of people also hold the belief.
Religious believers might claim that the fact in this case would
be God's opinion on the matter. A relativist, however, would
claim that there are no real moral facts – so moral propositions
cannot be true; there are simply expressions of opinion.

Plato's theory provides a solution to this quandary.

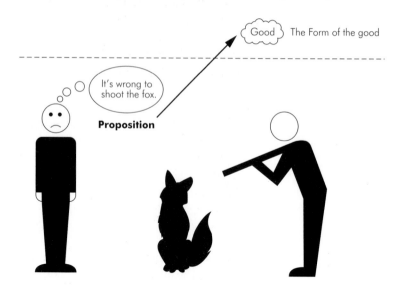

Here the onlooker is claiming that it is wrong to kill the fox. In Plato's theory another world of Forms exists alongside the physical world. In this world of Forms exists the Form of the good, and knowledge of this Form would reveal the relevant fact in relation to shooting the fox. The Forms exist independently of human thought, so the truth of the proposition will be independent of human thought; in other words it will be objective.

So Plato's theory shows a way in which moral truths can exist and hence a way in which the relativist can be defeated.

Criticisms of the theory of Forms

Although we cannot be certain of the exact nature of Plato's theory of Forms, we can be fairly certain that the theory represents the first systematic account to explain the nature of the physical world in relation to the mental world of ideas. As the first theory, however, we should expect Plato's ideas to be open to a fair amount of criticism. This section highlights some of the major flaws in the theory of Forms, flaws that eventually led Plato to reject his own theory.

Relationship between Forms and objects

The first major difficulty is this: if the world of Forms, as apprehended by thought, and the world of objects, as perceived by the senses, are so very different, then what exactly is the relationship between the two? There are various possibilities.

a) *There is no relationship.* If this is so, then of what use is knowledge of the world of Forms? Plato makes out that this knowledge is of some use; otherwise the philosopher-kings would be genuinely useless. So we can probably dismiss this account. But if there is a relationship between the two distinct worlds, then what is it?

b) *Objects participate/partake in the Forms.* In this interpretation the objects in the world actually contain some of the Forms and it is this that defines what the object is. In the same way perhaps as all wet objects are wet in virtue of having some water on them, all dogs are dogs in virtue of having some of the Form of dogness. This is problematic though, for if a pretty flower literally contains some of the Form of beauty (and presumably some of the Form of ugliness) then the Form of beauty itself is no longer a singular thing. There are lots of little Forms of beauty in things. Plato, however, does not seem to imply this, as he frequently stresses how each Form is singular and unique, not scattered throughout the world of objects. Also for some Forms the idea of an object partaking of the Form doesn't make much sense. One can imagine a pencil being a pencil in virtue of containing a certain amount of the Form of pencilness; however, consider a large pencil. In this case the pencil would have a certain amount of pencilness contained within it but would also have a certain amount of the Form of largeness too. However, it is less easy to see what this might involve. On the surface it seems the large pencil would just have more of the stuff needed to make a small pencil. It's hard to see how the Form of largeness could be residing in the shape somehow, as this is the same for both the large and the small pencil and it's also hard to see how it could be residing in the physical stuff, as again this is the same for the large and the small. Quite how a large pencil physically partakes of the Form of largeness is difficult to imagine.

c) *The Forms are like patterns for objects.* In this view two different beautiful flowers are both beautiful in virtue of the fact that they resemble the blueprint of beauty represented in the Form of beauty itself. Much of the language of the *Republic* suggests that this is how Plato conceived of the relationship between the Forms and objects in the world. However, this account also presents some philosophical difficulties, the chief one being that the theory leads to an INFINITE REGRESS, a criticism that has become known as Aristotle's THIRD MAN ARGUMENT.

Aristotle's third man argument

What counts as Aristotle's third man argument is not universally agreed and its effectiveness is also widely debated. Plato himself puts forward a version of the argument in one of his later dialogues, the *Parmenides,* and Aristotle also gives a version in his book the *Metaphysics.* Aristotle uses the example of a 'man' in his account – hence the term the 'third man argument'. However, below is the version given by Plato, which involves the concept of large.

All large things can be said to be large in virtue of the fact that they possess a property that resembles the Form of largeness. So one might imagine a collective set of all the large things in the world; what links all the things in the set is the fact that they have a property that resembles the Form of largeness. So Forms are what link a group of particular objects with a certain property. However, surely the Form of largeness also has this property? If yes, then we have a new group of things; all the large physical objects in the world (1) and the Form of largeness itself (2). The question then arises as to what links all the members of this new group. Presumably it is another Form – as Forms account for the similarities between objects. Perhaps one might call this third Form the 'Form of the Form of largeness'. But this new Form must also have the property of largeness, so will join all the large things and the Form of largeness in the new grouping; and we need a new Form to account for the similarity of the objects in this new grouping, and so on.

The theory of Forms suggests you need to resort to big X (a Form) to explain why all the little xs in the world are similar. In other words you need a new element to explain the similarity between the little elements. However, if this is the case why should we stop here? For we still have a similarity between little elements and the big elements that needs explaining; what makes these similar? Presumably it's that they resemble some third element, perhaps a super-big X, and so on. The claim is that we need to introduce a third element then a fourth then a fifth and so on, and that the theory leads to an infinite regress.

An analogy might help to explain the point. Imagine a child, Eve, has lots of farmyard animals and you are trying to get her to pick out the cows. There are only two cows mixed in with all the pigs, chickens, horses and goats so the task is not an easy one. You might pick up one of the cows (cow 1) and ask Eve to find the other cow. Imagine though that Eve fails to pick out cow 2. What you might do instead is get a giant stereotypical model of a cow (cow 3 – the Form of a cow) and then ask Eve to find any animals that resemble this big new cow. But would this work? According to the third man argument it is bound logically to fail as if it did work it would lead to an infinite regress. To see what this infinite regress involves let's imagine that the stereotypical cow device works and see what this implies. Remember that Eve was unable to see the similarity between two cows (cow 1 and cow 2), but the introduction of the big cow (cow 3) somehow worked and she was then able to see the similarity between the particular cows (1 and 2) by seeing the resemblance to the big cow (cow 3 – Form of the cow). But if you need to introduce a third cow to reveal the similarity between the first two this seems to imply we need a fourth cow. To recap we needed cow 3 to see the similarity between 1 and 2; but, if this is so, how was Eve able to see the similarity between 1 and 3 (the Form of the cow)? Here we have a case of two objects, the cow and the Form of the cow, accordingly we would need the introduction of a new cow (4) so that Eve can see the similarity between 1 and 3 too by comparing it to the new cow (4). But even this won't help, for in order for this to work we would need to introduce another cow (5) so that Eve could see the similarity between cows 3 and 4, and so on.

The general point is that if Eve was unable to see the similarity between two cows the introduction of a third does not help the matter. We will still be left with the problem of seeing the similarity between certain objects and we will keep needing to introduce a third object to overcome this. This problem repeats itself forever, which in philosophical language is termed an infinite regress.

■ **Figure 3.6**
Unable to see the similarity between two cows

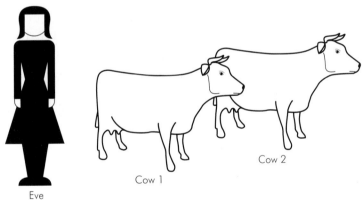

Eve

Cow 1

Cow 2

■ **Figure 3.7**
Might introducing a third cow help?

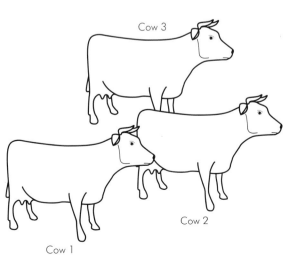

Cow 3

Cow 2

Eve

Cow 1

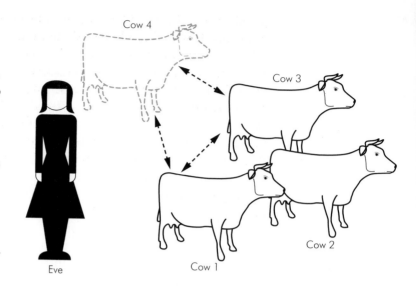

**■ Figure 3.8
Introducing a third
cow does not solve
the problem**
If Eve is unable to see the
resemblance between two
cows (1 and 2) then
introducing a third cow
can't help as Eve will still
need to see the
resemblance between two
cows – this time 1 and 3.
Might we need cow 4 to
see this? And so on ...

Cow 4

Cow 3

Cow 2

Cow 1

Eve

This example uses the idea of a child knowing (an epistemic
example), whereas the third man argument simply uses the
example of an object's being (an ontological example) but the
analogy still holds. If two cows are cows only in virtue of
resembling a third cow, the Form of a cow, then we are still
left with the problem of what unites the Form of a cow and
the individual cows – presumably that they all resemble the
Form of the Form of a cow, and so on.

Do all objects resemble their Forms?
The philosopher Wittgenstein suggests that we use certain
terms to apply to the world in a way that doesn't allow for a
simple definition. Consider the example of the word 'game'.
There are many different games in the world, ranging from
the Olympic Games to crosswords to hide and seek. If one
tried to give a definition of a game, there would always be
certain games that fell outside of this definition. For example,
not all games involve competition or bats and balls. The
relationship between all the games in the world is a complex
one and one that does not admit to a simple explanation.

The following analogy is often used to illustrate this point.
Imagine a photograph of a large family. Certain members of
the family will have features in common: Uncle Bob may have
a similar nose to cousin Danny, and Aunty Betsy might have
similar hair to Grandma Williams. However, there will be no
single feature or set of features that all of them have. The
people in the photo can be said to have a 'family
resemblance'. This idea can also be applied to certain general
terms. Many of the different games in the world will have
certain elements in common: some might involve bats, others
nets, but there is not single feature or set of features that they
all have. Games, taken as a whole, can be said to have a

'family resemblance'. This presents a problem for the theory of Forms. It would imply that there cannot be a single Form of a game that can be the pattern for all games, as this pattern will contain a set of features, and some games will not contain these features. In Plato's defence he might argue that if they do not resemble the Form of a game then they are not really games at all. However, Wittgenstein and others might argue that this represents a misunderstanding of how words work. It is up to humans how we use the word 'game' and this does not depend on any resemblance with these allegedly existing Forms.

Silly Forms

Another problem with Plato's theory of Forms is the problem of silly Forms. Again Plato recognises this in his later dialogues. It is all well and good to talk about the Form of justice, beauty, love and the good. But what about the Form of toenails or of spitefulness or egg fried rice? If we take on board all these Forms, and Plato gives us no good reason why we shouldn't, the theory of Forms starts to look a little silly. We must also remember how Plato chooses his examples of Forms to suit his theory. They are all relative qualities or moral ones. It is a lot harder to support his theory if other examples are chosen. Plato himself in the dialogue the *Parmenides* casts doubt on the existence of the Forms such as mud, dirt and hair; however, the theory of Forms cannot really be picky as to which Forms it allows. If there is no Form of hair then what is it that unites all the various examples of hair in the world? And if we can do without a Form of hair, why not also dispense with a Form of beauty or justice?

Misunderstanding of how language works

Language itself throws up some difficult philosophical questions. One of the biggest questions is how does language work? How do words and sentences portray meanings and communicate ideas?

Introspection does not appear to give us clear answers to these questions. Whilst you are reading these words, try to focus on what is going on in your mind. Is there a flurry of images? Is an 'inner voice' translating the printed words into spoken words, or perhaps directly into thoughts? Perhaps you are not aware of any process, it is as though you are simply looking at the words and simultaneously understanding their meaning. The answer is not clear, but what is clear is that understanding has taken place (hopefully!).

Theories of language attempt to give an account of how language works and one of the earliest and most obvious accounts goes something like this.

Consider the following sentence.

Jane's dog was wearing that spotty hat again.

Here the word 'Jane' is about a specific person, 'Jane's dog' is about a specific animal and the 'spotted hat' is about a specific hat. Given this, it seems natural to conclude that words and phrases somehow stand for or refer to things in the world. And, because words stand for things, language enables us to talk about them when they are not present. However, this theory soon runs into difficulties when we start to consider the nature of *universal* terms, that is terms which do not refer to individual things.

To see the problem consider first abstract nouns such as the following:

- love
- justice
- truth
- beauty.

What kinds of thing could words such as these stand for? Is love a thing in the world, like a dog? Can we suppose beauty to be an object like a hat? If not, what are we talking about when we use words such as these? We seem to be able to use and understand these and similar words without difficulty, but how can this be if we don't know what they refer to? This problem of the 'missing object' does not just apply to abstract nouns, but also to everyday general terms such as:

- tree
- dog
- shoe.

Which tree does the word 'tree' refer to? Surely it cannot stand for any particular tree, since we use it to refer to many different trees. Does it then refer to all trees? But then how is it we can talk meaningfully about trees that no longer exist, such as the trees used to build Noah's ark, trees that haven't yet been planted, or non-existent trees, such as the imaginary ones that might grow on the moon? Perhaps then the word doesn't refer to any actual trees, but to a kind of idealised tree or the idea of a tree in the mind.

The problem of how universals and general terms work has vexed many a philosopher over the years and to some extent is still a current philosophical issue. We can see that something akin to Plato's theory of Forms could help to solve some of these issues and this has led some commentators to claim that it is precisely this issue that underpins the core of Plato's famous theory.

However, theories as to how words work have changed considerably over time, such that the view that words stand for objects is no longer universally held. This has led to the claim that Plato might have based his theory of Forms on a misunderstanding of how language works.

A full account of the criticisms underpinning this view would involve a lengthy detour into the philosophy of language which it is not possible to make in this book. However some of the ideas undermining this position are as follows:

Word/object relationship is wrong

Not all words stand for objects. What objects do the following words stand for: 'of', 'to', 'in', 'the', 'minus'? This is related to the criticism below.

The sentence is the unit of meaning

An individual letter such as 's' has no meaning on its own. It is also claimed that this applies to words, as sentences are the smallest unit of meaning. Consider this, does the word 'apple' have a meaning outside of a sentence? Imagine a man walking down the road repeatedly saying the word 'apple', what would he mean? Perhaps that he is selling apples? He wants some apples? He is seeing apples everywhere? He needs to remember to buy some apples? Simply saying the word 'apple' repeatedly does not seem to be meaningful, as it is not a proper sentence. Sentences such as 'I want an apple', or 'apples are great' have meaning. Plato's theory gives an account of the meaning of words, but this is not the point. We need to understand the meaning of sentences and to do this involves understanding the contexts and situations they are used in.

Words do not have meanings attached to them

The philosopher Wittgenstein rejects the idea that words have a mental idea or meaning attached to them. To understand how language works, he claims, is simply to be able to use it, and this does not involve grasping any 'idea' or 'Form' that might accompany a word.

How do we gain knowledge of the Forms?

A final criticism of the theory of Forms is that it is not entirely clear how one could gain knowledge of them. This question will be addressed in more detail later when we examine the similes of the line and cave (pages 143 and 153). As discussed earlier, Plato thought that the route to truth was through the process of arguing and reasoning, which he termed the dialectic. The suggestion is that a thinker might start debating and discussing the notion of, say, beauty; different ideas are explored and dismissed; eventually the thinker homes in on the truth. In terms of Plato's theory the thinker eventually grasps the Form of beauty. So the Forms are grasped or apprehended through a process of reasoning. However, quite how this is achieved and what it feels like to apprehend a Form remain unclear. This criticism leads us to discuss the broader question of Plato's theory of knowledge.

■ **Figure 3.9**
Reasoning leading to the grasping of a Form

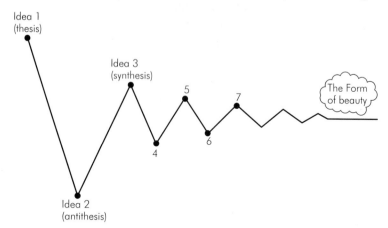

Plato's theory of knowledge 1 – extended analysis

These days when we think about what is involved in knowing something, we do not immediately think of someone grasping a universal or Form. It is true that a skilled surgeon, for example, will have a clear general idea of what the kidney is and of how it works, and this will guide her in performing an operation; but at the same time her knowledge of anatomy is something which is built on experience rather than theoretical contemplation. And in general we think of knowledge as the result of an accumulation of facts and information, rather than intellectual reflection.

In this light, Plato's conception of the essence of true knowledge may appear a little unfamiliar. However, one reason for this may be that he was starting from a very different everyday concept of knowledge from our own.

■ Difference 1

A common distinction made by contemporary philosophers, and one that fits fairly closely to our everyday concept, is between three types of knowledge:

A) knowing that
B) knowing of (acquaintance)
C) knowing how.

A) Knowing that, or propositional knowledge
For example:

I know *that* 2 and 2 is 4.
I know *that* Paris is the capital of France.

Knowledge *that* is usually concerned with facts and is the sort of knowledge tested in pub quizzes and the like. This kind of knowledge is usually of the form 'I know *that* ...' and is also called propositional knowledge. (A proposition is a sentence that asserts something about the world; other types of sentences such as 'Shut that door' or 'How are you?' don't actually assert anything.)

Because the knowledge claimed here is always of the kind that can be asserted in a proposition, the knowledge is solely language based. In recent times, when people talk about 'having knowledge' or 'knowing something', more often than not this is the sort of knowledge they have in mind. But it is not, however, the only kind of knowledge.

B) Knowing of (acquaintance)
For example:

I know Finbar Good.
I know Bristol well.

This is the kind of knowledge you claim when you have met someone or are personally familiar with an object or place. In these cases you know the person or place not through reading or listening or acquiring facts, but through direct acquaintance, having met the person or spent time in the place. Hence this kind of knowledge is often termed knowledge by acquaintance.

C) Knowing how
For example:

I know *how* to drive a car.
I know *how* to tie my laces.

This is the kind of knowledge you claim when you are proficient at something. Such knowledge is often thought about as having acquired a skill or ability. Because such knowledge is often bound up with movement of the body it is often hard to translate into propositional knowledge.

ACTIVITY Know how v. know that
Try writing an account of how to tie your shoelaces, so that someone who had never tied shoelaces before would be able to follow the instructions.

In English we use the word 'know' for each of the three types of knowledge mentioned above. However, other languages, such as French, delineate these kinds of knowledge more clearly:

1 *savoir* (knowing that)
2 *connaître* (knowing of)
3 *savoir faire* (knowing how).

Some philosophers would claim that we don't really need all three categories of knowledge, proposing that all of the categories could be reduced into one. For example, some claim that knowledge by acquaintance really boils down to propositional knowledge: when I claim to know Bristol what I really mean is that I know *that* it is situated by the River Avon; *that* City Road connects to Campbell Street; *that* the number 5 bus takes you to Clifton, and so on. In other words, knowledge by acquaintance really just consists of a collection of propositional knowledge.

Behaviourist philosophers would claim that all knowledge is really know *how*. They claim that having propositional knowledge and knowledge by acquaintance are really just ways of doing different things, answering questions for example.

The exact nature of the different categories of knowledge is a philosophical dispute for another day. The key point to note is that these categories of knowledge are not set in stone. Indeed they have changed over time and were certainly not as clearly defined in ancient Greece.

ACTIVITY
1 Which kind of knowledge do you think you have the most of? Think of all the things you are actually able to do.
2 Which kind of knowledge do you think dogs have?

The Greeks did not make any clear distinction between these three types of knowledge. One reason for this is that the people considered to have expert knowledge in a field were generally craftsmen. They would have a working knowledge of the objects they dealt with, in the sense that we may say that a horseman knows his horses, a cook knows his onions or a carpenter knows his wood, and so on. On this model, knowledge is bound up with dealing with objects: something which involves being well *acquainted* with them, knowing *how* to manipulate them as well as possessing a few *facts* about them.

Understanding that knowledge in ancient Greece was centred around objects is helpful in understanding key passages in the *Republic*. As we shall see later, Plato distinguishes different types of epistemic states, from illusion to belief to full knowledge, entirely on the basis of the different kinds of object the mind deals with in each case. For more on this see page 143, the simile of the line.

Understanding the object-centred nature of the Greek concept of knowledge can also help make Plato's theory of Forms more comprehensible. Consider ordinary objects. When I see a red apple there is an object, namely an apple, which my mind is apprehending. When I see a beautiful flower, again there is an object that my mind apprehends, namely the beautiful flower. However, when I discuss the idea of beauty itself, what object does my mind apprehend? Because, for the Greeks, knowledge was bound up with objects, it makes sense for Plato to claim that when the mind has knowledge of abstract concepts it is likewise still apprehending objects, in this case conceptual objects. So higher types of knowledge, for example knowledge of beauty or justice, still have corresponding objects attached. We can see how Plato's Forms fulfil exactly this role. To know about beauty is to be acquainted with the actual Form of beauty. Concrete knowledge centres around concrete objects, so it might seem reasonable to assume that abstract knowledge must centre around abstract objects.

So we can see that, from an understanding of the Greek concept of knowledge, Plato's theory of Forms does not seem so strange after all – in fact it seems a natural step to take.

Difference 2

Another difference between the concept of knowledge used by Plato and the one in use today lies in the kinds of truth/object that can count as being worthy of the word 'knowledge'.

Today we happily apply the word 'knowledge' to facts that are both CONTINGENT and NECESSARY:

Contingent truths

Contingent truths are truths that could well have been otherwise: for example, the fact that Tony Blair was Prime Minister in December 2005. After all, he might have lost the election earlier that year, or might have resigned or been assassinated. There are many other possibilities that could have happened. Consider also that Chelsea won the Premiership in 2005/6. Again, although they won by a clear margin, it was never the case that they would necessarily win. A few extra losses along the way might have seen another team win the title. Contingent truths – of which the world generates millions of new ones every day – are only true because of specific circumstances within the world. They are also usually time bound – for example, it might be true (at time of writing) that Tony Blair is now Prime Minister but it will not always be true that Tony Blair is Prime Minister. Indeed it was never true before 1997.

Necessary truths

Some truths are not dependent on the specific circumstances of the world. They would be true regardless of whether events differed or not. For example, $2 + 2 = 4$ will be true regardless of anything that happens in this world. It will be true in any other world for that matter. Consider the claim that water is H_2O. Again this truth does not seem to depend on any specific circumstances. Wherever you are in the universe and you find water you will find H_2O, as they are one and the same thing. Necessary truths are true come what may; and will be true of all worlds. They are also true for all time, without having to add any dates on. It makes little sense to say that water was H_2O on 19 June 1968. Water always was H_2O and always will be.

ACTIVITY   Consider the following claims for truth. Decide in each case whether the claim, if true, would be contingently or necessarily true.

1 The Beatles had 19 UK number one singles.
2 Murder is wrong.
3 Newton came up with the theory of gravity.
4 A bachelor is an unmarried man.
5 Mercury is heavier than carbon.
6 Yellow and blue when mixed make green.

Today we are happy to use the term 'knowledge' for both contingent and necessary truths. For example I can *know* that both George Clooney and Christian Bale have played Batman on the big screen (contingently true) and I can *know* that the circumference of a circle will be approximately 3.142 times the diameter (necessarily true). The verb 'to know' sits quite happily in both these cases.

Plato, however, seems to be reserving the word 'knowledge' for necessary truths only. Plato would not count as knowledge all the contingent facts and trivia about the world, such as the colour of someone's eyes or the number of chairs in a given room, or the length of Socrates' hair on a given day. All these facts are contingent. Plato seemed to use the term knowledge for truths that have either a timeless or universal nature, such as the relationship between a diameter and circumference of a circle, or whether murder is right or wrong. Again, this is understandable as Plato's theory of knowledge is based on his theory of Forms. For Plato, we may look at beautiful things in the world and argue about which is more beautiful. However, we shall never have knowledge of beautiful things until we have apprehended or grasped the Form of beauty. This Form of beauty, according to Plato, is something that exists independently of the world and is timeless and changeless. In other words knowledge of the Form of beauty would be knowledge of a necessary truth.

Summary of Plato's theory of Forms and theory of knowledge

Initially it may appear that the theory of Forms is somewhat bizarre, in particular the idea that quasi-concepts can have some sort of existence independent of human minds. However it is only really possible to understand Plato's theory of Forms (his ontology) alongside his theory of knowledge (his epistemology). We have seen that the Greek concept of knowledge was primarily object-based. So it might seem natural for Plato that the possibility of conceptual knowledge would require there to be conceptual objects that the mind could apprehend. The Forms are exactly this – a kind of quasi-conceptual object. We can see that the Forms existing separately from this ever-changing world also allowed for the possibility of timeless, unchanging knowledge. Plato, perhaps inspired by the seemingly certain and unchanging truths of maths, saw this as the template for all true knowledge.

Back to those sight lovers

After this lengthy detour, we will now return to the text and explore section 476c–d.

Summary of the argument (476c–d)

> **Read** 476c–d

- (476c–d) The person who recognises beautiful things but denies the reality of beauty-as-such is like someone dreaming; while someone who can apprehend its Form is like someone who is awake. This is because to dream is to confuse an appearance for the reality it resembles. And sensible instances of beauty are appearances which resemble the Form of beauty. The non-dreamer recognises both beauty-as-such, and objects' participation (*metechein*) in it. Socrates now concludes that the understanding of the dreamer (the lover-of-sights) is one of belief or opinion (*doxa*),[18] while that of the non-dreamer (the lover-of-wisdom or the 'philosopher') is one of knowledge (*episteme*).

Interpretation

As we have seen, Plato reckons that the natural rulers of the perfect state are lovers-of-wisdom. But different groups of people love wisdom in different ways and Plato wanted to distinguish between the so-called sight lovers and the true philosophers. We are told that justice and beauty are singular and that philosophers love these single things that lie behind the many. In other words the philosophers seek knowledge of the Forms that lie beyond the world of the senses. Sight lovers prefer the individual occurrences of beauty that occur in the visible world, they are not interested in what links these instances together or what they share or 'participate' in. Sight lovers can thus offer no account as to what beauty itself is, and even deny the existence of the Forms.[19] For this reason they do not possess knowledge, but only opinion (*doxa*) and in a key simile Plato likens their understanding to that of a dream. This simile of the lover-of-sights' apprehension of the world is important in that it suggests that sense experience involves the apprehension of a world of mere appearance, a world which resembles reality and which is often mistaken for reality, but which is in fact a kind of illusion.

■ **Figure 3.10**
The difference between lovers-of-wisdom and lovers-of-sight

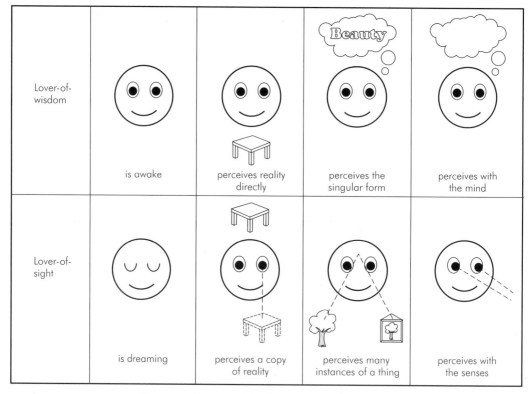

Lover-of-wisdom	is awake	perceives reality directly	perceives the singular form	perceives with the mind
Lover-of-sight	is dreaming	perceives a copy of reality	perceives many instances of a thing	perceives with the senses

Socrates has said that those who do not already accept that Forms are distinct from particular things that partake of them will need convincing (476a). And so now he produces further arguments in support of the contention that the understanding of the lover-of-sights involves a different faculty (*dynamis*) to that of the philosopher. Now read the argument from 476e–478e where Socrates develops the idea that knowledge concerns what truly is, namely the Forms, and that the world of physical things can only ever be an object of belief.

Summary of the argument (476e–478e)

Read 476e–478e

- (476e–477a) Knowledge has to do with what *is*, and ignorance (*amathia*) with what *is not*.
- (477b–478b) Faculties can be defined as powers we possess by which we apprehend objects, for example sight or hearing. Faculties are distinguished by their objects (or 'fields') and by their effects. Opinion and knowledge are faculties and as such they have types of object which are peculiar to them.
- (478b–e) Opinion lies 'between' knowledge and ignorance since it is clearer than ignorance but darker than knowledge. So if there is something which is 'between' 'being' and 'not-being', i.e. between what is and what is not, it will be the object of opinion.
- (478e–480e) In the final sections of Book 5 Socrates is concerned to find what it is that lies 'between' 'being' and 'not-being' in order to identify the proper objects of opinion. By arguing that sensible things fit the bill the conclusion can be drawn that the lover-of-sights is a lover of opinion and not a genuine lover-of-wisdom. Only the philosopher is concerned with knowledge, i.e. with what *is*, namely the Forms (see the argument from opposites on page 97 below).

■ **Figure 3.11**
The differing clarity of knowledge, opinion and ignorance

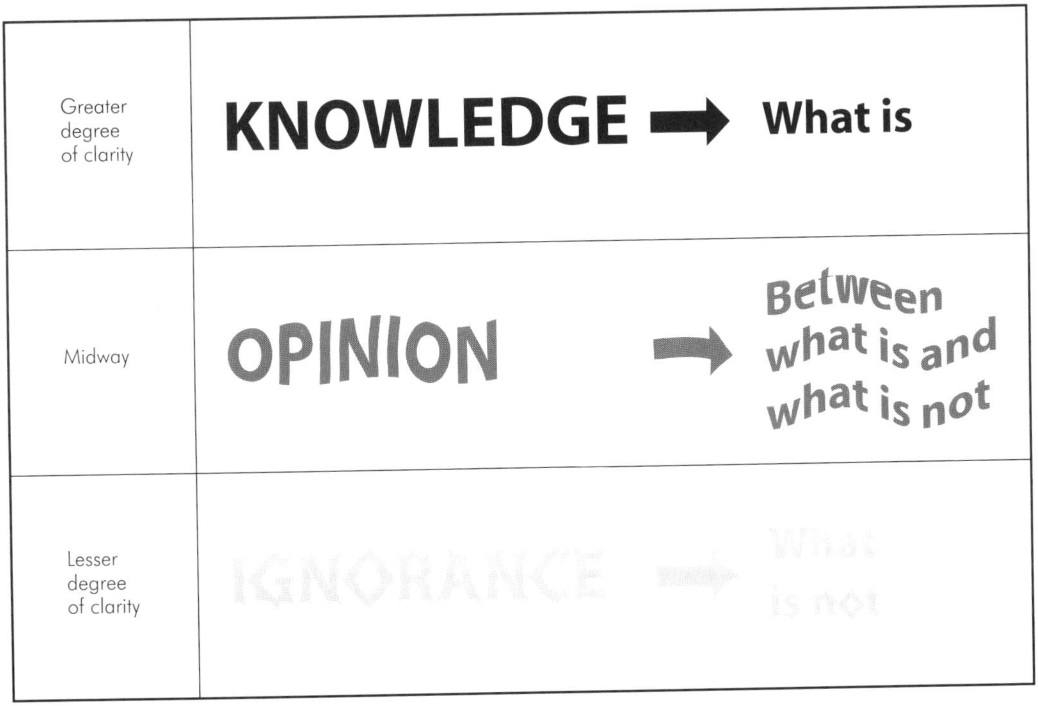

Greater degree of clarity	**KNOWLEDGE** ➡ **What is**
Midway	**OPINION** ➡ Between what is and what is not
Lesser degree of clarity	IGNORANCE ➡ What is not

Since knowledge is about what is, and ignorance is about what is not, opinion which is between knowledge and ignorance must concern whatever lies between what is and what is not. And this, as we see in more detail below, is the physical world.

Interpretation and evaluation

more difficult

■ What *is* and what *is not*

Socrates begins the argument by saying that since knowledge is related to what *is*, then ignorance – i.e. that which *is not* knowledge – must be related to what *is not*; and this allows him to make the further claim that opinion concerns what both *is* and *is not*. So it seems we are going to need to get clear about what he means by what *is* and what *is not* if we are to make sense of these difficult passages. Now, initially it seems to make a certain sense to say that knowledge is about what *is*, for if I know the rose on my desk (in the sense of being acquainted with it) then my knowledge does indeed concern something which 'is', namely the rose. And similarly, if I genuinely know certain facts about it, for example that it is red, the rose must exist and must really be red.

▶ criticism ◀

However, what exactly can it mean for ignorance to be related to what is not? Surely if I don't know the rose, having never encountered it, then this doesn't mean my state of mind is about a nonexistent rose, but rather that it is not related to anything. Similarly, if I don't know that it is red, or mistakenly believe it is red when in reality it is pink, and so am ignorant of a certain fact about it, then it sounds equally odd to say that my ignorance is about a rose which is not. Moreover, it sounds even stranger to suppose that opinion concerns a peculiar world lying somewhere between what exists and what does not, for surely things either exist or they don't. There can be no half-existent things.

The oddness of Plato's approach perhaps arises from his tendency to view knowledge as the apprehension of an object, on the model of how a craftsman knows his material. Since knowledge must successfully grasp something which actually does exist, being in general is thought to be the proper object of knowledge. And since ignorance involves a failure to grasp anything it must be about what is not or 'not-being'. However, rather than reify what doesn't exist in this way as the peculiar object of ignorance, wouldn't it be more reasonable to conclude that ignorance is not related to anything? A state of ignorance seems best characterised as a failure properly to grasp an object, rather than the grasping of a non-object. In other words, that which is not knowledge would be that which fails to relate to anything, rather than that which relates to nothing. So if I am not acquainted with a rose or do not know that it is red, this simply means that my state of mind is not related to anything in reality. Perhaps Plato has been seduced by language – much like the Cyclops in the *Odyssey*[20] – into supposing that the expression 'that which is not' refers to a special kind of thing. And note that if Plato had taken the route of supposing that ignorance doesn't relate to anything he might have gone on to reason that opinion relates to the same object as knowledge – namely that which is – but that it does so imperfectly. And this may well have been preferable to the strange notion that the objects of opinion must have a particular degree of existence, somewhere between what is and what is not.

However, perhaps we are being too hasty and Plato has something else in mind. So far we have supposed that Plato means by 'what is' that which has actual existence. But the Greek word *einai* does not distinguish between the English expressions 'to exist', 'to be true', and 'to be something or other' (e.g. beautiful, just, etc.), that is to say, between the EXISTENTIAL, VERIDICAL or PREDICATIVE uses of the verb 'to be'. These distinctions may best be clarified through some examples.

Take first the sentence:

> There is a cow in the field.

Here 'is' is used to mean that there *exists* a cow, and so is termed the *existential* use of the word. This is the usage we have assumed so far in understanding Plato to mean that knowledge concerns what *exists*.

The second possible usage of the Greek *einai*, which isn't readily rendered in English simply by the verb 'to be', asserts that some claim *is* true, as when we might say:

> The claim that Mount Olympus is in Greece *is true*.

This is termed the veridical use of the verb 'to be'.

Now take a third example:

> That balloon is green.

In this sentence the word 'is' indicates that the balloon has a particular property, namely the colour green. This is known as the *predicative* or *descriptive* sense of *is*, because 'predicate' is the term for a word or phrase that ascribes a property to an object.

Now, what we have so far seen is that it is difficult to make sense of Plato's thinking if he has the existential use in mind since it sounds like nonsense to say that ignorance is of what doesn't exist, and even more odd to talk of opinion being about what both exists and does not exist. So perhaps he has the veridical use in mind and intends to argue that knowledge is of what is *true* and ignorance of what is *false*. Such an interpretation has some initial plausibility since it suggests that I will have knowledge when what I claim to know is true, and ignorance when it is false. Perhaps Plato's intention is to suggest that being ignorant is believing something which is false. So the example would be of my believing the rose is red when it is not. In this case my opinion doesn't match reality, and so it is about something which 'is not' in the sense of 'is not true'.

▶ criticism ◀ However, while this interpretation is fine when it comes to knowledge and ignorance, it is difficult to square with Plato's comments about opinion. For what can it mean to say that opinion concerns what lies between truth and falsehood? Certainly, opinions may be *either* true or false, but this is not quite the same as saying that they lie between the two. Either the rose is red or it isn't and my opinion may be true or false. But it must be one or the other, not a bit of both. Also, since on this interpretation ignorance is defined in terms of its object not being true, and knowledge in terms of its being true, then false opinion would be the same as ignorance, and true opinion the same as knowledge. But having no place for the key concept of opinion makes a nonsense of this interpretation of Plato.

Given the difficulties with the veridical interpretation, let's look at the third use of 'is', and explore the possibility that Plato is saying that knowledge involves truly judging something to have a particular property, that is, truly recognising that, for example, something is red or beautiful. On this reading, his claim would be that one can only *know* that a rose is red, to the extent that it really *is* red, and genuinely to know something is to know that a property can be truly ascribed to it.[21] At the same time being ignorant of something would involve not being able to ascribe properties to it, for example if I didn't know what colour the rose was, my state of mind would be about something which *is not* red. This way of reading Plato fits better with the later move, which we will be examining below, where he argues that knowledge can only be of what fully is, for example, red or beautiful, and that those things that are only ever qualifiedly such and such, namely physical things, can only be the objects of opinion (see the argument from opposites below).

Whatever the merits of these different interpretations of
Plato's meaning, it is unlikely that Plato had any clear idea of
which of the three uses of '*einai*' he intended, and all three
doubtless have a part to play in his thinking. In reading these
passages it is best to try to stay alive to each of these different
threads in our efforts to appreciate and engage with the
development of his thought.

Distinguishing faculties

The principle that faculties are distinguished by their 'fields
and effects' is crucial to Plato's argument. Faculties are said to
be the same if they have to do with the same objects or
'fields' and have the same effects. Although the language
involved is a little confusing, the principle is fairly easy to
grasp. Consider how we might define the faculty of sight.
What, in other words, makes sight different from other
faculties? One answer would be the way in which it
apprehends its objects, in other words its 'effect', namely to
make things visible. Moreover it can be distinguished in terms
of the kinds of thing it deals with, in other words its 'field',
namely colours and shapes. And what distinguishes the faculty
of hearing? Again a plausible answer would be in terms of its
effect, or the way it works, namely to make things audible;
and in terms of its 'field' or proper objects, namely sounds.
So sight and hearing are different faculties precisely because
they have different fields and effects.

Plato applies the same kind of reasoning to distinguishing
knowledge and opinion. They too are regarded as faculties,
and they too can be distinguished from each other in terms of
the way they grasp an object, i.e. in terms of their effects.
Knowledge grasps its object infallibly, and opinion grasps its
object fallibly. Because knowledge and opinion do not have
the same effect, they cannot be the same faculty. And so the
conclusion is drawn (478a–b) that they must have to do with
different objects or fields. Plato concludes that, while
knowledge deals with being, opinion has to do with whatever
it is that lies between what is and what is not.

▶ criticism ◀ One objection to this line of reasoning is to point out that
knowledge and opinion might be distinguished in terms of
their effects alone, and not by their objects. Thus it could be
that opinion and knowledge have to do with the same things
and the difference consists only in the one being fallible and
the other infallible. Knowledge would involve the correct
ascription of the property of redness to my rose, for example.
This ascription would be infallible. However, an opinion that
my rose is red might be true, but would fall short of being
knowledge because there remains the possibility of error since

the manner in which the opinion has been arrived at is not infallible. Such a view is far closer to our intuitions concerning the difference between opinion or belief and knowledge. It is also closer to contemporary philosophical accounts which claim that knowledge is a special kind of belief, much in the way that reading is not a distinct ability from seeing, but a special kind of seeing.

Significantly, this type of analysis of knowledge accords well with Plato's own discussion of the topic elsewhere. In Book 10 (601b–602b), for example, he distinguishes the two by reference to use. The user of something has knowledge of it since he understands what makes it fulfil its function, whereas its maker only has true opinions about how to construct it. Knowledge here is to do with direct engagement with the object and an understanding of why it is as it is but, whether one has opinion or knowledge, the object remains the same. The *Theatetus* suggests knowledge may be 'true opinion with an account' and the *Meno* that 'having reasoning about the cause' may make true opinion amount to knowledge. In other words some kind of 'explanation' is required in addition to true opinion to convert it into knowledge. In these passages Plato's account is like modern accounts of the concept of knowledge which take it to consist of true belief or opinion plus some further element such as a justification or the right causal route to the acquisition of the belief. So the idea that opinion and knowledge have different objects is actually a rather unusual view. It is also one with radical implications, one in particular being that the philosopher inhabits a very different world from the ordinary citizen. This separation of the philosopher from the rest of us will make problematic Plato's contention that the philosopher is nevertheless the one who knows how to govern and direct other citizens in what is best for them, a difficulty we will be exploring further below.

■ Opinion is 'between' knowledge and ignorance

A pivotal claim Socrates makes in these passages is that opinion lies *between* knowledge and ignorance, but the precise sense in which this may be said to be so is not altogether clear. He says that knowledge is 'clearer' than ignorance, presumably meaning that opinion is more fallible than knowledge and less fallible than ignorance. When we know something we apprehend it without any possibility of being mistaken about it. By contrast when we are ignorant of something we fail to apprehend it at all or, in a sense, are totally mistaken about it, and opinion is 'intermediate between' these extremes.

► criticism ◄ However, even if we agree that opinion lies between ignorance and knowledge in respect of its clarity, it doesn't necessarily follow that its objects or fields must also be 'between' the objects of knowledge and ignorance, i.e. what is and what is not (478c–d). For the conclusion to follow, Plato needs to establish some sort of conceptual connection between the two axes of clarity/obscurity and being/not-being to show that intermediacy in the one case implies it in the other. After all, dusk is between night and day in respect of 'clarity' but it doesn't follow that crepuscular animals inhabit a nether world between what is and what is not.

The argument from opposites

more difficult

Plato thinks he has shown that the object of knowledge is what *is*; the object of ignorance what *is not*; and the object of opinion lies between these extremes. So if he can find something which both is and is not, that is to say something which lies between being and not-being, then he will have found the proper object of opinion. This is what he tries to do with the so-called argument from opposites.

Summary of the argument (479a–480)

Read 479a–480

■ (474c) We have seen Socrates argue that to love something is to love the whole of it without qualification.
■ (476e) We also saw that the lover-of-sights claims that there are 'many beautiful things', while the philosopher realises that there is only one thing which is truly beautiful, namely the Form of beauty itself.
■ (479a–d) Now Socrates returns to the lover-of-sights and points out that any particular instance of beauty, i.e. any beautiful thing, can equally well be said to be the opposite of beautiful. 'Particulars' (as opposed to universals) partake of both ugliness *and* beauty, justice *and* injustice, big *and* small, and so forth. In general, opposite epithets can be applied to any particular. Such things, therefore, can no more be said to be than not to be, and so should be placed between 'being' and 'not-being'. Since Socrates has shown that whatever lies between being and not-being will be the object of opinion (478e), sensible particulars must be objects of opinion.
■ (479e) Only the Form of beauty is beautiful without qualification, i.e. always beautiful and never ugly. A Form is a thing which, by contrast with sensible objects, bears a predicate without qualification. Since only the Forms can

be said to *be* without qualification, only they can be objects of knowledge.

■ (480) Thus the lover-of-sights loves opinion, and only the philosopher loves reality.

Interpretation

We have seen that for Plato the world perceived by the senses cannot be an object of knowledge. One of his reasons for this becomes clear in these passages, namely that it is too changeable and ambiguous. The qualities of objects of sense can only be ascribed to them with certain qualifications. In other words, such qualities are always dependent on other factors such as the state of the perceiver, the context, the time they are perceived and so forth. So, for example, the same act which is just in some circumstances, such as returning what is not one's own, will not be in others. This is part of the point made by Socrates in response to Cephalus' definition of justice in Book 1, when he argued that it may be unjust to return a weapon belonging to a madman. In Plato's words the particular act both *is* and *is not* just. In the 'argument from opposites' passage Plato makes the point by arguing that if a sensible object is termed 'beautiful' this is because it is beautiful in certain respects, relations or aspects, that is, subject to certain qualifications. The self-same object will also be the *opposite* of beautiful in some other respect. For example, no person could be said to be *perfectly* or *completely* beautiful. They might be beautiful to some, but not to others; or beautiful in their youth, but not when they are older; or beautiful in blue, but not in grey; a beautiful dancer, but not a beautiful singer; have beautiful eyes, but an ugly mouth, and so on. Plato concludes from the observation that we cannot say of a sensible object that it unqualifiedly *is* something or other, that is, that it has a certain quality such as beauty; we cannot be said to *know* that it has that quality. His thought here is that knowledge cannot admit of qualifications because it concerns only what *is*. What is *really* beautiful cannot also be ugly. What is truly just can never be unjust. So our particular judgements about beautiful things and just acts are simply opinions since they concern objects which lie 'between being and not-being'.

This notion is perhaps clearer if we consider that the model case of knowledge so far as Plato was concerned – i.e. knowledge of mathematical and geometric truths – does not admit of the kinds of qualification that claims about the physical world do. As we have seen, mathematics and geometry do not depend on physical reality for their validity since they deal with universals. Intelligible objects like circles and numbers do not exist in time or space and so cannot undergo any changes. By contrast even the most enduring of physical objects is both located in space and subject to change over time. This kind of consideration leads Plato to suppose that the science of mathematics attains to precision and certainty to the extent that it does *not* apply to objects of sense. And since he thinks it must nonetheless apply to something he posits a non-sensible or intelligible realm which is *more* real than this world of imperfect, 'qualified' objects.

Assuming for the moment that knowledge of qualities such as justice and beauty is possible – that is, that the same kind of precision is possible when dealing with ethical and aesthetic terms as with mathematical ones – it follows that such qualities must *be* without qualification. By reasoning by analogy with mathematics, Plato draws a parallel between the facts that we never encounter perfect or ideal circles and that we never behave perfectly justly, or enact perfectly just laws. But, the thought goes, if we are to reason about such things and acquire knowledge of them, we need to deal with ideal circles and with ideal justice, in other words, with the Form of justice. Only by dealing with universals can we hope for an understanding which is not qualified by the peculiarities of this or that time and place and people.

As we saw above (page 88), Plato does not count as knowledge our opinions about contingent facts and trivia about the world, such as knowledge concerning the colour of someone's eyes, the number of chairs in the next room, or the length of Socrates' hair on a given day. All these facts are contingent and so will cease one day to be the case. Rather he wanted to reserve the term 'knowledge' for truths that have a timeless and universal character, such as the relationship between the diameter and circumference of a circle.

Evaluation

▶ criticism ◀   A key difficulty concerns whether we are inclined to accept the theory of Forms which underpins the argument. We may admit that particulars can never bear their predicates in an unqualified way; but from this it does not follow that there must exist abstract objects, the Forms, which do. In other words, we can accept that no beautiful things can ever be perfectly beautiful, but deny that there must be something which is. While all beautiful things have something in common, this doesn't itself establish that there exists one thing 'beauty itself' independently of any beautiful things, which is unqualifiedly beautiful. Perhaps, on the contrary, there just is *no such thing* as an unqualified application of terms like 'beauty', etc.

▶ criticism ◀

Another important objection draws attention to the fact that in Book 5 Plato's discussion of the Forms deploys terms which have opposites (justice–injustice, beauty–ugliness, etc.). He does not use terms like 'red' or 'fish', which do not. And while we may say of some just act that from another point of view it is unjust, we cannot say of a particular fish that in certain contexts or perspectives it is not a fish. Either it is, or it isn't. So we have no reason to suppose that there are Forms for terms which do not have opposites. Thus Plato's argument does not exclude the possibility of knowledge of certain things which are not Forms, for example that the mackerel is a fish. And, it seems, he has not excluded certain sense particulars from being objects of knowledge, although later (as we shall see) he appears to suppose that he has.

In defence of Plato we might consider how a term such as 'fish' or 'red' might be said not to apply unqualifiedly to particulars. For example, in the case of a red rose, it's not red all over, in all lights, from any perspective, or for all time. Compared with a crimson carnation it might appear decidedly off-red and, even while admitting it is partially red, I must admit that it is also delicate, sweet smelling, and thorny – all further ways in which the rose is not simply red. And a particular mackerel will one day cease to be a fish, and will certainly not be perfectly fishlike in all respects – a less able swimmer than a herring perhaps.

Despite this, however, Plato does not argue in this way in the *Republic* and it does appear that we can object to the claim that we can only truly *know* what is unconditionally 'fishlike' or 'red'. Surely we can indeed know things about the physical world while admitting various qualifications. Knowing this is a fish, here and now, is still knowledge even though it is not eternally true. And I can know that it is a beautiful day even while admitting that its beauty is ephemeral.

Key points: Chapter 3

What you need to know about **philosophers and sight lovers**:

1 Philosophers are different from sight lovers in that the latter love the multiplicity of objects whereas the former love the single objects that lie behind the multiplicity.

2 Plato relies on his theory of Forms to support much of argumentation in the chapter. The theory suggests that in addition to the multitude of objects in the physical world there exists an intelligible realm of ideas that can explain similarities and differences between the objects in the world.

3 The concept of knowledge used by the Ancient Greeks is different from the concept of knowledge employed today.

4 Knowledge is related to what is (i.e. the Forms), ignorance to what is not, and belief half-way between.

Why philosophers should rule

Introduction

This chapter examines Plato's arguments for why philosophers would be good rulers. Plato puts forward a series of arguments to show that a philosopher (a lover-of-wisdom) would naturally have all of the other qualities desired in a leader. Having painted a very flattering picture of the philosopher, Plato then has to explain why the philosophers who actually exist in society are not held in such high regard. He attempts to explain their lowly status by presenting a simile of the navigator on a rowdy ship.

This chapter contains the following main sections:

- The desirability of the philosopher-kings
- The simile of the ship.

The desirability of the philosopher-kings

Summary of the argument (484a–487b)

Read 484a–487b

- (484a–e) Now that we have a preliminary understanding of who genuine philosophers are it is clear that they should rule the city state (*polis*). For only they are able to apprehend the models or PARADIGMS – the Forms – after which the state is to be patterned so that it most closely approximates to the ideal. The rulers must be those who know such realities, while also not being inferior to others either in practical experience or in any virtue.
- (485a–d) How can knowledge be combined with experience and virtue in the philosopher? Philosophers love all truth (see above 474c–475c) and hate untruth and therefore they will love everything 'akin' or 'closely connected' to truth, including wisdom.
- (485d–487a) The philosopher is less affected by bodily desires than other people because her desire is directed toward the truth, which is intelligible. Therefore she will be self-controlled and not covetous. Whoever contemplates all time and all being will not regard human life as of great importance and so will not be mean, cowardly or fearful of

death. Being of well-balanced mind she will not be motivated by desires that prevent her from being just. The philosophic character will be just and civilised from an early age. It will have a good memory, and the virtues of a sense of proportion, self-control and grace. If education and maturity are added to this natural disposition one has the ideal character to rule the state.

Interpretation and evaluation

■ Philosophers are wise

If philosophers have the capacity to grasp the eternal and immutable, while those who have no such capacity are not philosophers and are lost in multiplicity and change, which of the two should be in charge of the state? (484b)

After defining a philosopher Plato offers various reasons why these philosophers should be rulers. The first reason is contained in the quote above, namely that philosophers have knowledge of the Forms.

But is this a good reason? To answer this question it is worth considering an even more fundamental one. Why should any one have power over anyone else? What possible reasons could be given for why one person should be able to decide upon aspects of other people's lives? Since recorded history, and probably for a long time before, there have always been people in positions of power, and over the years various justifications for this situation have been put forward. Here are a few possibilities, as outlined in the following activity.

ACTIVITY Rank the following reasons in order of acceptability, i.e. put the most reasonable first.

I am justified in exercising power over others because:

1 God decrees it.
2 I am stronger than anyone else.
3 My army is stronger than anyone else's.
4 It is my birthright.
5 I am richer than any one else.
6 I have more knowledge than any one else.
7 I have been elected by the people.

Plato's suggestion for justifying power may be better than some of the others, but many people today would argue that the last reason – that I have been elected – is the most acceptable one. The thought here is that a person can only justifiably assume power over other people if that power has, in some sense, been given up by the people. In other words, the only just situation is one in which rulers acquire the consent of the people and are accountable to the people. Taking the perspective of the ruled in making decisions about who should govern did not become the focus of political thinking until a long time later than Plato, but today we tend to take it for granted that the rights of the ruled should take precedence over any virtues of the ruler. For Plato, writing the first ever work of political philosophy, the quest to find the most suitable ruler was approached by inquiring into who is best qualified. From this perspective it is understandable that Plato would single out wisdom as the defining quality of the ideal ruler. And while we might object that simply having knowledge cannot justify anyone in wielding power, it is still reasonable to ask whether it is a desirable characteristic to look for in a leader, and surely most would agree that we do not want our leaders to be stupid or ignorant.

■ Philosophers have all the other qualities desired in a leader

However, while being knowledgeable is clearly desirable in a leader, it is not the only characteristic. Plato now examines the philosophical character further in an attempt to show that the philosophers' knowledge means they will have other qualities which make them best suited for ruling. In these sections it is the *natural* temperament of the philosopher, not those traits that are developed through education (which are discussed in Books 4 and 7, and at 502c ff.), with which Plato is concerned. In essence Plato's strategy is to show that true philosophers naturally possess every kind of excellence or virtue and that such characteristics are required for virtuous and effective rule. He shows this by arguing in each case that if a philosopher had genuine knowledge they would also have the various other virtues. In what follows it is worth bearing in mind that the natural virtues that Plato discovers in the genuine philosopher are those that follow from the psychic harmony he identifies in the just soul. In Book 4 he tried to show that an individual is wise to the extent that the reasoning part of the soul rules and makes decisions on behalf of the soul as a whole (442c). Since reason is directed toward the truth, such a soul will love truth. The moderation and justice in the soul consists in the desiring part submitting to this rule, while courage consists in the spirited part being the ally of reason. What this means is that if rulers allow themselves to be controlled by their physical passions, or by the spirited part of their soul, then they cannot be good or just rulers. For if they do not act justly themselves it can only be because they don't know what justice is (since if someone knows what justice is then they will be just).

ACTIVITY

Read 485–487

Read 485–487 and try to identify the many qualities Plato claims are possessed by philosophers, as well as his reasons for thinking they must have them. In the table below we have noted each quality and the argument for why philosophers possess it.

How convincing do you find each of these arguments?

Quality	Where mentioned	Justification
1. Truthful	485c	A lover of the truth will not tolerate an untruth.
2. Shuns physical pleasure	485e	If someone's desires are set strongly in one direction they are correspondingly less strong in any other direction. So if someone is interested in pleasures of the mind they will not be interested in pleasures of the flesh.
3. Self-controlled with money	485e	Lack of desires will mean fewer concerns that need to be satisfied by money.
4. Not mean	486a	Someone who can grasp the important things in life, i.e. the Forms, will not worry about small and petty things.
5. Courageous	486b	Possessing knowledge involves recognising how insignificant you are in comparison to the vastness of the universe and thus you do not fear death and are brave.
6. Easy to deal with and just	486b	Lovers of knowledge will be well balanced, have no need to be boastful, cowardly or mean.
7. Finds learning easy	486c	Anyone who has succeeded in acquiring knowledge must have a natural propensity for it and not find it painful to acquire.
8. Good memory	486c	To acquire knowledge it is necessary to have a good memory.
9. Good taste	486d	Truth, like taste, is related to having a sense of proportion. Therefore a lover of truth will have good taste.

► criticism ◄

1 On the face of it, it seems reasonable to say that a lover of wisdom must love being truthful. However, we might wonder whether someone who enjoys the pursuit of truth in their academic life need also find it important to tell the truth to others in their political and social life. Moreover, Plato does not apply this principle evenly throughout the book. Earlier Plato suggests that the philosopher rulers might have a need for telling myths or fictions (*pseudos*) in order to ensure that the characters of the people are not corrupted and that they grow into morally upright citizens (377a ff.). Plato argues that 'spoken falsehood' (*pseudos*) can be useful 'as a kind of preventive medicine' (382c and 389b–c). Moreover he argues that the propagation of an elaborate foundation myth – a sort of lie, or piece of propaganda – will be necessary to ensure that all citizens do what is best for the community and stay loyal to it (414b–415d). Plato's discussion of this 'Noble Lie', which we discussed above (page 44), has often been criticised for valuing social cohesion above the truth, and as betraying an impulse to TOTALITARIANISM above the value of individual freedom of thought.

2 Consider whether it is really plausible that one could escape bodily desires through contemplation of the truth.

We may engage in contemplating the Forms but this cannot allow us to ignore the basic and particular requirements of life such as eating and sleeping. And while there may be some who are able to control their physical needs to a remarkable degree, it is not obvious that these are all lovers of wisdom in Plato's sense. Plato likens desire to a stream which can be diverted in different channels but we may question whether the analogy is apt. Might it not be the case that we have several streams of desire, each directed at different goals, so that increasing interest in one will not mean that the others dry up?

3 Even if you lacked physical desire and only sought knowledge, might you still not be tempted to recklessly spend your money on books, etc? Is recklessness in spending purely a result of the quantity of different desires, or might recklessness not also be the result of the quality of one very intense desire?

4 From any description of the universe, it is hard to argue that a certain attitude should therefore follow. I could also argue that the enormity of the universe might make me focus intently on those things very close to me that I can have control over. Might I not then become petty? (Also don't we want our leader to have an almost petty eye for detail?)

5 Again, as with number 4, Plato is moving from a fact about the universe, its size, to a suggestion of how we ought to feel. Such an argument is hard to justify. Might the sheer size of the universe and its grand timescale also make me want to hold onto the flickering candle of my life as tightly as I can?

6 This only follows if the other arguments work and establish that the leader is not mean or boastful, etc. Also someone with such vast knowledge might be quite tricky to get along with.

7 It might seem that a wise philosopher would find learning easy, almost by definition. But might they not find it difficult to learn but be driven to learn by other desires, such as the desire to do good? Also, might they enjoy the perverse pain of learning and so want to learn more – even though they find it difficult?

8 Is the sort of knowledge Plato has in mind all about memory? Some of the greatest minds of all time have been forgetful people.

9 Is good taste really about a sense of proportion? Surely what counts as good taste is purely relative to a society, and changes over time, like fashion? If no one else thinks philosophers have good taste then surely they don't?

Even if we accepted all of the arguments on page 105, it still would not prove that philosophers have the necessary qualities to rule, as Plato does not put forward any arguments to show that these are indeed qualities necessary for a good ruler. He simply assumes that the set outlined above are the qualities any leader should have (487e).

experimenting with ideas

1 Write your own list of qualities that you think a good leader should have.

2 Compare this list with Plato's.

Many people might include a number of other qualities such as being single minded, being a good communicator, or being able to listen to criticism. Also, some of the qualities outlined by Plato might not be on the list at all. After all, many might wonder whether anyone who could successfully conquer the fear of death, and so regard human life and common desires as unimportant, could truly understand and sympathise with his fellows. And such understanding and sympathy, it might be argued, would be essential to making a just statesman.

The simile of the ship

The philosophers outlined in the *Republic* are portrayed as some kind of super-humans, not only having vast knowledge but also possessing all the main virtues in abundance. However the reality of the philosophers in ancient Greece was somewhat different. Socrates, Plato and their fellow philosophers were considered quite odd by the rest of society and were certainly not held up as examples of super-humans. Quite the opposite: Socrates and Plato were frequently lampooned as weird eccentrics by the contemporary playwright Aristophanes. The picture of philosophers painted by Plato in the *Republic* seems quite at variance with the picture of philosophers perceived his fellow Athenians. The next section explores this difference of perceptions.

Summary of the argument (487b–489c)

Read 487b–489c

- (487b–487e) After learning that philosophers will have these amazing qualities, Adeimantus brings the conversation back down to earth by noting that if philosophers are so wonderful, how come in real life they are normally regarded as at best *useless* and often as positively *vicious* and *dangerous*. Philosophers, he says, are 'very odd birds, not to say thoroughly vicious; whilst even those who look the best of them are reduced by this study you praise so highly to complete uselessness as members of society' (487d). Surprisingly, Socrates agrees there is some truth in the charge of uselessness, but says that this is because true philosophers are not recognised by most people and so no use is made of them. He then proceeds to elaborate on why they are considered useless members of society through the use of an extended analogy. (He deals with the charge of being wicked and a danger at 489d ff.)

- (488a–489c) Socrates presents a parable to illustrate the plight of the genuine philosopher in contemporary society. Suppose there is a ship with a partially deaf and myopic captain and the crew are quarrelling over how to navigate and who should be at the helm, but none of them has any genuine skill in the art of navigation. Suppose also that one faction is able to take control of the ship by killing their rivals and drugging the captain. They would then turn the voyage into a pleasure cruise and admire the seamanship of whoever is able to control the captain. Meanwhile, the true navigator, with his knowledge of the seasons, winds and stars, is ignored and thought useless by the crew. The crew do not understand what true navigation consists of and if the navigator is useless it is because the other sailors fail to make use of him.

Interpretation

ACTIVITY Read the simile (488a–489c) and write down suggestions for what each of the following represents:

1 The ship
2 The captain
3 The crew
4 The navigator
5 The stars.

Democracy in Athens

To appreciate the simile fully we should remember what democracy was like in ancient Athens. Women and slaves could not vote. About 80 days a year people would gather at the Assembly and discuss the issues of the day, hear 'legal' cases and make decisions affecting the state. However, in practice only the rich, and usually the young and rich, could afford to take time off to attend. So the democracy was not fully representative of the society. In addition to this by all accounts the democracy was fairly corrupt. Generally, when discussing any issue, those people who had a reputation for being good at public speaking would be asked to give a speech (this is why sophists would train young men in the arts of public speaking, so as to increase their political power). These good speakers, who could easily be bribed, were usually more interested in power and wealth than in reason and principles and thus would make speeches to pander to the crowd. Also, when voting came around, people could be bribed to vote in a particular way. So meetings of the Assembly were not always ordered affairs but were quite chaotic, with groups and factions going around bribing, threatening and smooth-talking their way to influence decisions.

Interpretation of the simile of the ship

The simile of the ship represents this democracy in Athens. The captain represents the position of power, the crew the various factions trying to gain power, and the navigator represents the philosopher whose voice is lost or ignored. The whole business is chaotic and corrupt, much like the Assembly. In Athens the democratic politicians ignored the philosopher, as his skills were irrelevant to gaining the ear of the mob, and to gaining power. Money and rhetoric were the tools of influence, while reason and knowledge were almost irrelevant.

On the ship it is not that the navigator's skills are truly irrelevant – on the contrary, they are vital since he has the knowledge to guide the ship – it is just that the crew do not recognise this. The crew are more interested in the short-term pleasures of getting drunk, rather than in what is in the best interest of the ship as a whole. Likewise in the democracy the true philosopher has the necessary knowledge to run the state, but the others around him see this as irrelevant. And the democratic government is more interested in short-term pleasure and keeping power than in the genuine good of the state. Plato is suggesting that, yes, philosophers are considered to be useless members of society, but this is because society itself does not understand their true value. So we should not blame the *philosopher* for being of no use to the state, but rather those who fail to make use of him. The philosopher is not inclined to beg others to allow him to rule. For like the navigator he is concerned with the truth and not (like the crew) with the satisfaction of his immediate personal pleasures or with the acquisition of power.

This last point is a significant one as it looks forward to the contention (put forward at 519d–521b) that the only way in which the state will be well ruled is if it is ruled by people who don't *want* to rule but have something more desirable to do instead (i.e. philosophise). In other words, Plato believes it is of central importance that people don't get involved in politics for personal gain. For if people want to rule they will compete for positions of power and the state will be afflicted by internal conflict and strife, i.e. injustice – as is illustrated in the conflicts between crew members. (It is sometimes argued, as we shall see in more detail below, that this causes a difficulty for the possibility of Plato's state being realised, since those who are supposed to rule it wouldn't ever be inclined to do so.)

Note that alongside the critique of contemporary society's attitude to the philosopher, which Socrates makes explicit, is a critique of the way it organises the business of government. The democratic politicians attempt to secure power by seducing or doping the people and are not interested in the best way to govern, but only with, on the one hand, retaining power, and on the other hand, satisfying their immediate desires by turning their journey into a pleasure cruise. They are motivated by marginal interests and not by the good of the state as a whole.

Evaluation

If the argument is to succeed it must: (i) explain why philosophers appear useless and (ii) demonstrate that they are in reality useful. To evaluate its success in achieving these aims, we need to be aware that Plato is arguing, as he often does, through the use of analogy, and so the strength of his argument will depend on how similar the things being compared are.

■ Why do philosophers appear useless?

► criticism ◄

How well does Plato's analogy support the idea that philosophers appear useless because they are ignored by the scheming citizens? An initial point of weakness in the analogy is that on a ship a rowdy crew would surely still need a navigator even if they just wanted to turn the journey into a pleasure cruise. The navigator might still be considered *useful* even though he would not be regarded as leadership material. So, by analogy, philosophers should still be useful as advisors to those holding the power. And certainly it would seem likely that anyone in power could make good use of the knowledge of anyone who had reflected carefully on the nature of justice and who had understanding of the fundamental principles of good government. However, this does not seem to have been the attitude of the Athenians of Plato's day. Historians seem to agree that philosophers were indeed considered to be useless, their musings about life were parodied by the playwrights of the day, and philosophy was considered a fit subject only for a young man, rather than a grown-up politician. So why was this? One possible answer is that the philosophers' knowledge was actually too abstract and theoretical to be of any practical usé. Philosophers might sit around in idle discussion of how an ideal state might be run, but when it came to getting their hands dirty and engaging in the day-to-day business of actually doing it, they lacked the practical experience and common sense to get the job done.

Is there any support for Plato's suggestion that the perceived uselessness of philosophy was nothing to do with the abstract nature of the subject itself, but with the fact that the citizens of the Assembly did not respect or even see the need for logic and reason? Let's recall that politics in Plato's Athens was all about appealing to the masses to gain short-term power. Unpopular opinions, however rational, were ignored. The average citizen was very superstitious and likely to listen to rhetoric rather than examine rational arguments in a dispassionate manner. Indeed, if the rise of reason in the west was still in its infancy, it was largely due to Socrates and Plato that it started to gain a surer footing. Given all this, Plato does appear to have valid concerns about the state of Athenian democracy and it is likely that the philosopher, no matter how good his understanding of government might have been, would not have been seen as relevant to the scheming politicians in the Assembly.

■ Are philosophers really useful?

Even if we accept Plato's reasons for why philosophers were considered useless in Greek society, Plato still needs to show that they are in fact useful, otherwise their reputation is deserved.

▶ criticism ◀

In the analogy Plato is suggesting that the navigator, with his knowledge, should be running the ship and, in the same way, a philosopher, with his or her knowledge, should be running society. However, should the navigator really be running the ship? Perhaps, as we've already suggested, he would be a better advisor than captain. A leader requires other skills in addition to wisdom – courage, level-headedness, decisiveness and people-management skills are just as important – and yet the analogy does not imply that the navigator has any of these. So Plato's parallel fails to support the claim that the philosopher has all the skills required to be a leader. Perhaps the philosopher's perceived uselessness is justified.

We should note, however, in Plato's defence, that immediately proceeding the simile of the ship, Socrates tries to prove that a true philosopher would also have the required qualities of a leader, and so he can feel with some justice that this point is already proved, even though not well supported by the analogy.

■ Theoretical and practical knowledge

▶ criticism ◀

It is worth noting that, to the extent that Plato likens the philosopher to a skilled navigator, he must regard the ruler as having practical abilities and practical experience. And this means he looks to the Forms to gain not only abstract knowledge but also *practical* guidance, just as the navigator looks to the stars. This claim raises a question which is associated with the general problem of how Forms relate to particulars, namely whether it is really credible that knowledge of *universal* Forms could give one a better understanding of how to deal with the *particular* problems of government. How exactly does knowledge of the Forms enable the philosopher to rule? In other words, the question is whether the *practical* knowledge required of a ruler and the *theoretical* knowledge which is the province of the philosopher can really be brought together. And if, as Plato has claimed, every person is by nature best suited to a single task it would seem that those suited to making particular practical decisions in this world, and those suited to contemplation of universals, cannot be the same individuals.

In response Plato's idea may in part be that to have knowledge of what justice is in itself involves the understanding that any particular just act will of necessity only be just with certain qualifications. In the practical business of governing, any law, no matter how just, is bound in some respects to be unjust with regard to certain interest groups or in certain contexts, and so on. This is what Plato attempted to demonstrate in the argument from opposites. To enact laws must, therefore, involve weighing up a range of considerations to maximise justice while remaining alive to the fact that no law can embody justice absolutely. If a ruler is not aware of this, thereby *confusing* justice itself with particular just acts (as would the lover-of-sights), then that ruler would be inclined to suppose a particular law to embody justice absolutely. Clearly such a misunderstanding might well lead to social conflict and promote *injustice*. For if one is inclined to think that a particular law is *necessarily* just, or embodies justice without qualification, one might well be reluctant to change it if, for example, circumstances change.

■ Knowledge of facts and judgements of value

▶ criticism ◀ Another difficulty with the comparison is that it assumes the type of knowledge involved in navigation is equivalent to that involved in steering the ship of state. However, it can be argued that the two types of knowledge are very different. In the former case a navigator has the knowledge which enables him successfully to guide the ship from one port to another. This is a skill based on learning facts about the stars, tides, currents, the specifications of the ship, and so forth. However, knowing how to run the state is not a matter of knowing a lot of facts. Civil servants will supply politicians with the facts bearing on a situation, but the decision about what policy to adopt will not be determined by the facts alone. Rather, political decisions necessarily involve judgements of *value*. They depend on certain views about how we ought to live, which policies are morally right, and what society we want to work towards. Now, many would argue that there can be no objective basis for determining which of such judgements are correct. There is no universally discoverable body of knowledge which will tell us how we ought to run a state, and so government cannot be a skill like navigation.

This point rests on a distinction between facts and values, or the navigator's DESCRIPTIVE knowledge of facts, and the politician's PRESCRIPTIVE judgements.[22] However, Plato would reject this distinction. For on his view it is possible to have genuine descriptive knowledge of the Form of the good; in other words, it is possible to acquire objective and universal knowledge of the ultimate source of moral value, in terms of which all moral judgements can be deemed correct or incorrect. If a philosopher had knowledge of this then he or she would know how we *ought* to live and so the boundary between prescriptive and descriptive knowledge dissolves. So in Plato's way of thinking the analogy between philosopher and navigator is perfectly appropriate: both have objective knowledge of how to guide their fellows to what is in their true best interests. However, in accepting the analogy we must accept the theory of Forms and in particular the commitment to the possibility of objective knowledge of what is good. And if we have reason to doubt this, the argument fails.

■ The critique of democracy

As well as being concerned with the role of the philosopher in society, the parable of the ship also represents an attack on democracy in general. Part of the point Plato is making is that the skills required to gain control of a ship – such as pitiless self-interest; the ability to persuade, intimidate and manipulate others; being good at lying and deceit – are not the types of skill we would want our captain to have. Similarly the kinds of characters who are likely to rise to the top in a democracy – such as those with ruthless ambition; those able successfully to manipulate others through bribes, flattery or threats; those able to sway a crowd with persuasive oratory; and those with the tendency to make short-term populist decisions – are not those we actually want to be our leaders.

The crux of this argument is that in a democracy the skills required to *become* a leader are never the skills desired *in* a leader. Democracies do not produce the leaders we want and they never will. Many people think this is a powerful criticism of democracy and one that is not confined to the democracy of ancient Athens.

ACTIVITY

1 Consider the skills that are necessary to become a leader in today's media driven society. Make a list of the main ones.
2 Are these the skills that we want in our leaders?
3 Are democracies good at producing the right leaders? Is there a better way?

The *Republic*, in part, is a criticism of Athenian democracy. Plato's critique may be directed at the democracy of Athens, but his argument that appealing to the masses is not the way to ensure we have the best leaders represents an important difficulty for any supporter of modern-day democracies. Wouldn't we be better off choosing our leaders according to their aptitude for government, rather than on the basis of their looks, charm and the effectiveness of their election campaigns? We will be returning to this question when we examine the simile of the beast below (page 116).

As a final point, it is worth noting that as an *argument* the simile of the ship is not particularly effective since it begs Adeimantus' question of whether the philosopher is an expert in running affairs of state. That is to say, it presupposes as established what it purports to demonstrate. The analogy can hardly prove this, since if we are not already persuaded we will reject the assumption that the analogy is apt. It is therefore perhaps best regarded simply as an *illustration* of how it is possible for the philosopher to be (in fact) useless to the running of the state, while nonetheless being (in principle) the best person to rule.

Key points: Chapter 4

What you need to know about **why philosophers should rule**:

1 As well as having the required knowledge Socrates argues that philosophers will naturally have all the other qualities desired in the leader. Amongst other qualities he argues that philosophers will be truthful, self-controlled, generous, courageous, easy to deal with and have good taste.

2 Socrates argues that all these desired qualities will follow naturally from the wisdom of the philosophers. However much of the argumentation in this section is not very strong, and further Socrates does not argue the case that the qualities a philosopher would naturally have are in fact the qualities desired in the leader.

3 Adeimantus points out that Socrates' glowing account of philosophers is at odds with their public perception, claiming that they are considered useless and vicious.

4 Socrates agrees that the philosophers in their current society do appear useless but suggests that is because society does not know how to employ them properly. He argues this point through the simile of the ship which compares the way a navigator is ignored by a ship's rowdy crew to the way a philosopher is ignored in society.

5 The simile is open to several criticisms, notably that the knowledge required of the navigator is of a different kind to the knowledge required by a philosopher/ruler and so the comparison is not accurate.

6 The simile of the ship also serves as a criticism of Athenian democracy, suggesting that the current system will not produce desirable leaders, merely those who are able to manipulate a rowdy mob.

5

The simile of the wild and dangerous animal

Introduction

Earlier we saw Adeimantus claim that philosophers were useless and vicious. The simile of the ship defended philosophers against the charge of uselessness; this chapter examines Plato's defence against the charge that philosophers are vicious. Part of Plato's defence involves distinguishing philosophers from sophists, which he does by using another simile: that of the wild and dangerous animal. Plato then examines whether there is any hope for philosophers in society given their lowly status.

This chapter contains the following main sections:

- The simile of the wild and dangerous animal
- The plight of the philosopher.

The simile of the wild and dangerous animal

Having dealt with the objection that philosophers are useless, Socrates needs now to turn to the complaint that in contemporary society those who pursue philosophy into adulthood are often far worse than useless and can be a positive danger to society because of their vicious ways.

Summary of the argument (489d–493e)

Read 489d–493e

- (489d–491a) Socrates' response to the charge that philosophers are bad or vicious tries to show that philosophy cannot be responsible. For to love truth, as has been shown, is to be of good character. So how is this to be squared with the idea that most philosophers in contemporary society are wicked? Socrates' explanation is that on the one hand many philosophical natures are corrupted; and, on the other hand, many characters unsuited to philosophy imitate philosophers. Both these need to be examined in turn.

- (491b–492a) It is rare for someone to be born with the natural qualities to make a philosopher. But, paradoxically, it is these very qualities (e.g. courage, self-discipline, etc.) which make them prone to corruption, along with many of the good things in life (such as good looks, wealth and good connections). To explain his meaning, Socrates uses an analogy. A plant requires a good environment, such as soil and climate, in which to grow; and the more robust the plant, the more any lack of the proper environment will hinder its progress. In the same way, a strong natural character is likely to be particularly badly affected by bad upbringing, and so those with good natural qualities are at risk of becoming particularly wicked and dangerous.
- (492b–493a) A philosophical nature is corrupted less by the teachings of any individual sophist than by the bad influence of the public. The praise and blame heaped on philosophers by the crowd represents too great a pressure and many come to conform to public opinion. Worse, those who are not persuaded may be threatened with punishments (such as disfranchisement, fines or death). These pressures are such that for a character to develop perfectly in contemporary society would be miraculous.
- (493a–493e) Sophists don't teach genuine knowledge, but simply reflect conventional opinions. The public is like a large and powerful animal. Rulers in contemporary society, like the animal's trainer, pander to its moods and wants without concern for what is truly good. They can, through long experience, acquire a knack (*techne*) of prediction and control of the behaviour of the multitude, but they cannot provide a *rational account* (*logos*) of this behaviour. Consequently their understanding of how to treat the animal does not constitute *knowledge* – it is not a science – but merely a deftness at pandering to the demands of public opinion.

Interpretation

Socrates is here responding to Adeimantus' complaint that philosophers are not just useless, but also thoroughly vicious, contrary to how Socrates has painted them. We've followed Socrates' explanation of why they appear useless, through the analogy of the ship, and now he offers a two-fold explanation for why they appear vicious. The first reason is that would-be philosophers must be naturally gifted and so are bound to be the focus of attention from the crowd in any public meeting. A young person's heart is bound to be moved by the efforts of the crowd to influence them and it is almost inevitable that they be 'carried away with the stream' (492c) of social pressures and adopt the opinions of the crowd. Although corrupted, the natural talents of such a person mean that they are likely to be successful in whatever they do, and so they may well be particularly effective in pursuit of their corrupt ends.

Secondly, and more importantly, philosophers can have a reputation for being vicious because the public confuse them with the sophists and it is the sophists that really give philosophy a bad name. Hence it is the sophists, not the philosophers, who are truly vicious. To explain what is the matter with the sophists Socrates offers another simile, this time involving a wild animal.

ACTIVITY   Read through the simile of the wild animal (493a–493d) and think about the following questions.

1 What does the animal represent?
2 What does the trainer represent?
3 What is wrong with the trainer's method of handling the animal?
4 How does the simile relate to Athenian democracy?
5 Can you see any parallels with modern politics and politicians?

Plato outlines two contrasting ways in which a trainer might treat his animal. The first way is simply to study the mood of the animal, its likes and dislikes, and then to provide it with what it wants in order to please it. This method may keep the animal happy in the short term, but the trainer would have no real knowledge of the animal's needs or of what is in its best interests.

The second way would be to make a proper study of the animal's nature: its physiology, natural habitat, diet and so forth. Armed with such knowledge the animal might then be looked after and trained according to its best interest. The first way would never improve the animal's health or fitness whereas the second way would.

By implication, Plato is arguing that there are also two ways of running society. The first is the way of the sophist. The sophist trains young men for public life by teaching them how to make popular speeches, how to read a crowd and judge what to say. Young men trained in sophistry would then go on to gain power in the Assembly, expertly making speeches designed for mass appeal and so keeping the crowds happy. The sophists called their understanding of human emotions a science and this is what they offered to teach. But Plato is claiming that sophists simply react to the demands of the crowd and give the public what they want. And this is not at all the same as knowing what the public needs or what is good for them. A politician trained by a sophist has simply learned to pander to the populist taste and has no real understanding of what is in the true interest of society.

A philosopher, on the other hand, would have genuine knowledge of human nature and would know what is genuinely good for human beings and for society. He would thus rule in everyone's interest, much in the way that a parent knows what is in the interest of a child. Simply giving a child what it wants on demand would not be in the child's interest and not the right thing to do. And in the same way, a good leader does not respond to whatever the people happen to expect, but makes policy on the basis of what is genuinely for the best.

Evaluation

Paternalism and freedom

Modern political theorists call Plato's thesis a form of 'paternalism', i.e. the view that because our leaders know what is in our best interest, they should be allowed to make laws accordingly. Since J. S. Mill's essay *On Liberty* (1869) paternalism in governments has been increasingly attacked. Mill's view is that an individual should be left to decide what is good for him or her; a government should only make laws preventing individuals from causing harm to others. Each individual should be taken to be the best judge of his or her own best interests and no government should enact laws in the supposed interest of individuals without their consent. He preaches that freedom from interference is the best way to achieve a happy society.

Mill's approach has been influential and his 'harm to others' principle, or some variant of it, is regarded as a truism within the political discourse of the liberal consensus in the west today. For example, the arguments for banning smoking in confined public places are thought to have force because it has been shown to cause harm to others. But any attempts to justify banning it altogether are likely to encounter stiff opposition, in part because it offends against Mill's principle.

Now, although this principle is not consistently applied – for example it can be argued that the individual should be free to take recreational drugs, such as cannabis, since doing so does not cause harm to others – the authorities in western liberal democracies tend to claim that personal freedom from meddling governments makes for a happier society. If this view is right then Plato's approach in the *Republic* is entirely wrong. Governments should not act on our behalf in our 'best interests', but rather leave us to our own devices.

However, not all philosophers agree with Mill. It may be argued, for example, that being free from interference is worth nothing unless a person has genuine and real options for choosing the life they want to live. If you have no money, are uneducated and starving, then being free from the interference of others is not particularly important or desirable. Critics claim that negative freedom, that is to say freedom from interference, is not the real freedom we should be pursuing. Positive freedom, in other words, having genuine options available to one, is far more significant. Only through access to education, libraries, leisure facilities and a health service, for example, can we be free to pursue our genuine desires. Providing these requires governments to 'interfere' more in our lives; to tax some of us highly and to make decisions which will serve our best long-term interest. But without such interference any freedom we may possess is worthless. Proponents of positive freedom argue that a more paternalistic approach from the government actually provides the conditions under which the people can be liberated.

■ Two styles of leadership

Plato's analogy with the trainer of an animal also differentiates two styles of leadership which still have relevance today. One type, what we will call the 'responsive' leader, listens to the public and is prepared to change policy as the national mood changes. By contrast the 'resolute' leader will ignore shifts in the popular mood and stick to the path that they believe is right. Which approach is better? There seems to be a recognition in contemporary society of the advantages of both. To form a policy without consultation and ignore the views of those affected is often regarded as the worst kind of dogmatic intransigence. So, the argument goes, it is good for leaders to be sensitive to the desires of the people. However, this approach can also be accused of weakness. According to this counter-argument, strength of conviction is the key virtue in a leader. It is their job to lead, and this will mean that they have, from time to time, to make tough and unpopular decisions.

These opposed arguments reflect a tension in what we expect of our leaders. On the one hand, we want governments to listen and respect the voice of the people, yet, on the other hand, we want them to take a longer-term view and act in our best interest. In systems in which politicians are to some degree accountable to the people, perhaps inevitably, some compromise must be found between the two. As regards Plato's position that the ruler should have no concern for the whims of the people, the principal argument against it is based on the idea that it is integral to a just system of government that the people be involved in the decisions that affect them. Even if the people do make mistakes this doesn't mean that they have no moral right to control their own destinies.

Democracy

The simile also represents, of course, a further attack on democratic forms of government. Plato is claiming that a democracy will inevitably lead to the type of leadership typified by the trainer of the wild animal. It leads to populism, which is a bad thing because the public do not know what is in their own interest. However, it might be objected that Plato is missing the point of what real justice is about. Even if society does not know what is in its best interest, people still have a right to self-determination. The right to choose your government is more important than a government making a better decision on your behalf.

How democratic, though, do we really want to be? In the UK at the moment, for example, we have a form of representative democracy where the population is divided into constituencies consisting of about 70,000 voters who elect a single person to act and vote on their behalf in Parliament. However, the technologies now exist to allow us to bypass the need for representative MPs and return to a form of direct democracy, as they had in ancient Greece. This would not involve a return to smaller city states, since we could, in principle, vote on a daily basis on each specific issue as it arose, for example by pressing the red button on TV remote controls or by texting using mobile phones. Decisions could be instantly made by the general public and each decision would be a true reflection of the will of the people.

ACTIVITY
1 Would transforming the UK into a direct democracy be a good idea?
2 What difficulties can you imagine?

Possible difficulties of a direct democracy

- Policy would not be coherent. If you were a diplomat dealing with a country with this form of democracy, then you might be concerned that it might change its policy from one moment to the next making it very difficult to negotiate with.
- People might be more interested in short-term benefits. Most people are in favour of lowering taxes, but if we lower taxes too far, the state would not have the revenues to function.
- People might be more interested in their own self or class interest than in the interests of the state as a whole.

In a direct democracy, some issues might be too complex for the people to understand and make informed decisions about. Imagine if the following proposals were put to the general public.

■ Ban the Qur'an.
■ Bring back hanging.
■ Shorten the working week to three days.
■ Reduce unemployment benefit.
■ Allow all pubs to stay open all night.
■ Spend more money on the health service.

1 What do you think the public at large would vote for?
2 What impact would these decisions have?

In thinking about the case of direct democracy, we may be more sympathetic to the force of Plato's arguments. Simply giving the people what they want is not always in the best interest of society, so perhaps it is better for wiser people to rule. However, it might be argued that Plato's arguments have less force against representative democracy in which there are various checks and controls on how the will of the people is translated into policy. Again, this may suggest that we need to find a middle way between the chaos of a direct democracy and the repression of Plato's paternalism.

Further criticisms of the simile of the wild animal

■ Not comparing like with like

▶ criticism ◀

This analogy, like that of the ship, can be accused of not comparing like with like. Science, being descriptive, may well have some claim to know which food and living conditions are in the interests of an animal's health. But the knowledge of what is in a society's interest is a different matter. Here we enter the world of prescription. As we have seen, it can be argued that it is impossible to acquire objective knowledge of matters of value and so the best we can hope for are opinions about the correct way to run society.

However, as with the simile of the ship, Plato's defence would be that knowledge of the Form of the good is possible, so a philosopher ruler could genuinely claim to know what is in the interest of society, just as a vet may know what is in the interest of an animal, and so the simile is apt after all. Again this defence only works if we accept Plato's theory of Forms.

Plato's view of humankind

► criticism ◄ It is also worth noting that in the analogy Plato compares the people to a *wild* and *dangerous* animal. This may be taken to reveal something about Plato's attitude to the ordinary citizens of Athens. They are not, on his view, a sophisticated, civilised or thoughtful bunch. They act on instinct, pursue their base desires, and don't concern themselves with the good of society. It has been said that if you know a political philosopher's opinion of human nature then you can work out their political theory without having to read it. And there certainly seems to be some truth to this saying in Plato's case. If Plato really had such a low opinion of the ordinary citizens then we can understand why he thought democracy was bad and why philosophers should rule. But there is no real defence of the assumption that the majority of people must behave in this way.

Nature v. nurture

► criticism ◄ This leads us to another line of objection to Plato. His arguments assume that the ordinary people are incapable of making rational decisions about issues of social policy. Now, even if we accept that this may have been true in Athens, it does not follow that this must always be the case. Plato clearly believes in the natural inequality of human beings (e.g. 370a–c), and this is part and parcel of his definition of justice and the notion that each individual should work in the field to which he or she is *naturally* or *essentially* suited. What is 'natural', as opposed to 'conventional', for Plato equates with the Form or essence of something. The ideal state is itself thought of as the 'natural' state, for it is the state in which different types of people do what is 'natural' to them. What is 'conventional' is at best a copy of this ideal or essential nature. His argument that the just city should be ruled by an elite group of the wise depends on this view of the natural aptitudes of different types of people. One might therefore object that as a matter of fact people's aptitudes are not pre-determined along genetic lines, but are forged by their education. It may be that through proper education *all* the people can be brought to the state where they become capable of making informed choices about policy. Modern representative democracies have shown, it may be argued, that it is possible for ordinary citizens to look beyond their own self-interest when voting, and to deliberate rationally about their choice, and this might be a model for how a direct democracy might be made to work without degenerating into chaos.

The simile of the wild and dangerous animal

Earlier we saw Adeimantus claim that philosophers were useless and vicious. We have now seen how Socrates has answered these claims; in the first case by suggesting that society does not know how to use philosophers, in the second case by arguing that philosophers are confused with sophists. Given their low standing in public opinion, Plato's vision of a state ruled by the philosophers seems a highly unlikely occurrence. In the next section Socrates examines whether and how a philosopher might ever become a ruler.

The plight of the philosopher

Summary of the argument (494–504d)

Read 494–504d

- (494a–496a) The multitude of common people cannot apprehend the true beings (the Forms) and so cannot understand the worth of philosophy. Consequently they will inevitably try to sway someone of philosophical character away from philosophy. Paradoxically, the very superiority of the philosophical nature is an aggravating cause of its falling away from philosophy. For the ordinary people will hope to use such a superior nature for their own ends. And the natural philosopher will succumb to flattery, pride and ambition. A corrupted philosopher – because naturally gifted – can inflict greater injustices on the state than ordinary people. (Cf. the plant analogy at 491d.) The abandonment of philosophy leaves the way open for unworthy people of lesser natures (namely sophists) to masquerade as philosophers and give philosophy a bad name.
- (496a–497a) In cities as they actually are, philosophers are not permitted to fulfil their natural function, namely to rule. It is fortuitous that all philosophical natures are not corrupted, and that anyone at all becomes able to occupy him or herself with philosophy. Those who are so able avoid involvement in the running of states and try to keep themselves free from the wickedness they perceive around them.
- (497a–499a) No existing city is congenial to the philosophical nature except the ideal city. Once founded, our city will need to contain people (namely philosophers) who understand the rationale or principle (*logos*) on which it is based (484c–d). The improper use of philosophy, however, will be perilous to the city. Thus, in order to judge how a city might encourage the proper use of philosophy we need to decide the correct age for studying it. Socrates recommends that philosophy not be studied until the soul is mature. And there must be encouragement for the disposition to seek the truth for its own sake.

- (499a–500b) No perfect man or city will arise until either philosophers become rulers or rulers become philosophers. The implausibility of the notion that they should rule is brought about by impostors.
- (500b–e) The philosopher will attempt to order himself and the city according to the rational order of the Forms and make it moderate, just and excellent. Given this, the many will realise the necessity of rule by philosophers for their own happiness.
- (501a–502c) In order to fashion the just state the philosopher rulers would need to begin with a state and human character which have been wiped clean. Only on such a clean slate or canvas can the philosopher hope to model the citizens after justice, moderation, beauty and so forth. This will help persuade the citizens of the possibility of the city. And if it is possible it is best.
- (502c–504d) We have shown (i) that the rulers must be philosophers, (ii) how they are to be selected from childhood, and (iii) that they must be both quick-witted and have stability of mind in order to be educable. Now we must see how the rulers are to be tested and educated.

Interpretation and evaluation

Can Plato's ideal state ever become a reality? In these passages Plato makes clear that his utopia is supposed to be a possible model for a real-life state to emulate. And yet he recognises the unlikelihood either of a philosopher becoming a ruler, or a ruler becoming a philosopher. Philosophers, after all, have no interest in politics, so it will be hard to persuade them to get involved. Moreover, the people will not recognise the need for philosophical rule, and so are unlikely even to try to persuade them. Plato's own experience of trying to educate Prince Dionysius of Syracuse must have made him very aware of some of the difficulties involved.

▶ criticism ◀

One particular difficulty with the process of realising such a state is that the people involved, be they rulers or ordinary citizens, must take on roles for which they cannot have been adequately prepared. Those taking on the roles of ruler won't have been brought up in the ideal way, since the ideal society didn't then exist; and those being ruled, similarly, will have been used to a different system, and so all are unlikely to be happy to accept their allotted functions. Plato talks blithely of the need for the artist of the new state to 'wipe the slate of human society and human habits clean' (501a) before fashioning the new order; yet how this cleansing might be effected is left unexplored: the possible human cost of any genuine effort to eradicate the influence of the past is truly horrifying – the Cambodian experience of the Khmer Rouge may serve as one example of the abuses such thinking may lead to. If we reckon wiping the slate clean to be a moral impossibility, then it may be that we must resist any attempt to set it up out of hand.

▶ criticism ◀ There is some conflict between the claim (at 499d–500b) that most people will be persuaded that rule by philosophers is a good idea and the claim that, if philosophers came to rule, the rest of the city, being unfamiliar with reasoned argument, would have to be 'compelled' to obey (499a–b). In effect, in order to appreciate that they are better off being governed by philosophers, the masses would have to accept that equality, freedom and self-government are worthless illusions. They would need to come to an understanding that civil liberties are not necessary if the rulers are truly just; and that what is needed is security and prosperity, rather than self-government and political freedom. But how can acceptance of this be assured if the non-philosophical multitude does not have knowledge of what justice is, in other words, if they disagree (rightly or wrongly) with Plato's definition? This difficulty is compounded by the fact that no attention is being paid to their pleasures. Surely in such a situation the people are likely to revolt? Although Socrates professes to think that the people could be persuaded by the same sorts of considerations as he has put forward so far (499e–500a), in part to meet this difficulty elsewhere, as we have seen, he argues that it will be necessary for the rulers to *deceive* them (389b and 414b–c). Some form of deception or propaganda – the Noble Lie – will be necessary to ensure political stability. As he points out, philosophy used improperly is risky (497d). In other words, what the people are permitted to know needs to be carefully controlled. Perhaps such indoctrination would work to control the masses, but whether or not we would regard this as 'just' is another matter.

▶ criticism ◀ It is worth raising once again the concern we touched on before of whether Plato, by debarring certain sections of the citizenry from any share in government, isn't thereby depriving them of an essential freedom which one might take to be integral to true justice. In other words is despotism, however benevolent or enlightened, always wrong? By defining people by their social function is Plato missing something crucial about what it is to be a citizen? Such questions readily lead into further concerns about the purity of the leaders' motives. It is often said that power corrupts and it is surely reasonable to question whether Plato's safeguards, namely his education system and not permitting his guardians any property ownership, are foolproof. Can we be sure that a group of philosopher rulers holding absolute power will remain enlightened and disinterested, or is it more likely, given what we know of human nature, that they would be tempted to abuse their situation and use their power to service their own self-interest? This is certainly the way history suggests tyrants behave, and might this not be because it is in the nature of power to corrupt, rather than that no philosopher has ever held the reins of power?

▶ criticism ◀   It is important to note that Plato's notion of citizenship (that is, those individuals who are to count as members of his three classes) does not encompass all the people living within the city. The remark at 469c makes clear that he envisages the existence of slaves, so long as they are not Greek. Note also that in the ensuing discussion about war Socrates argues that, properly speaking, conflict between different Greek cities should not be termed *war* since it is really an internal conflict between 'natural friends'. War properly so called is an external conflict between Greeks and non-Greeks or 'barbarians'. The suggestion is that *war* can be prosecuted more radically than should conflict between Greeks. The implication of these points is that the values Plato hopes to inculcate in his new state are relevant only to a limited class of people, namely Greeks. Slaves within the city, and barbarians without, are not accorded the same moral status. Recognising this fact about Plato's thinking gives us further reason to be concerned about his ideal state. For if our consciences have been exercised about the citizens' loss of power in Plato's paternalistic system, how much more concerned should we be for the disenfranchised barbarians. Plato's tribalism, it may be claimed, runs counter to the universalist claims made for his ideal city-state.

Key points: Chapter 5

What you need to know about **the simile of the wild and dangerous animal**:

1 Socrates argues that philosophers are perceived as vicious because they are often corrupted when young and also because they are confused with sophists.

2 The problem with the sophists is that they only have knowledge of popular opinion whereas philosophers have genuine knowledge of the world. Sophistry in government would not improve the lot of society whereas a philosopher, knowing the truth, could make a difference. This point is argued through the simile of the wild and dangerous animal.

3 The simile also represents an attack on democracy. It suggests that giving the public what they want (via a democratic process) is not in the best interest of the public. Because the public lack the relevant knowledge they do not know what their own best interest consists of and would be better off ruled by someone with expertise in this area. This argument is open to several criticisms notably the contemporary claim that the public have a **right** to self-government even if such self-governance is not in their own best interest.

4 Despite the difficulties facing philosophers in society owing to their poor public perception, it is still possible for a philosopher to become a ruler.

The simile of the sun

Introduction

Having argued that philosophers should be the rulers, largely on the basis that they have genuine knowledge, Plato turns his attention to the most important thing the philosopher should know: the Form of the good. This chapter explores what Plato means by 'the good' and examines the simile of the sun, which is presented to aid our understanding.

This chapter contains the following main sections:

- The good
- The simile of the sun.

The good

For Plato there are three principal evils afflicting political life in Greece: first, internal conflict; second, the unsuitability of the rulers for ruling; and third, its system of education. It is not only required of those who would construct the ideal state that they be philosophers, but also required of those who would maintain it. So the enduring stability of the state depends on the proper education of the young, and the system of education must be designed to protect the philosophers from corruption. In order to prevent bogus philosophers (sophists) influencing the young, teachers need to be carefully selected. This means that education cannot be left in the hands of individual caprice, but must be the responsibility of the state. However, before turning in earnest to sketch his vision of the pedagogical system within his ideal state (521ff.), Plato digresses to investigate the nature of the study of philosophy which will prepare his guardians for power. In so doing he provides an account of the ultimate goal of philosophy which is to attain knowledge of the Form of the *good*. The nature of the good and the quest for knowledge of it is the subject of the remainder of the sections we will be studying.

Summary of the argument (504d–506b)

Read 504d–506b

- (504d–505a) The most important study for the rulers has not yet been discussed and it has as its object the Form of the good. For all things are only useful, beneficial or good in virtue of their relation to the good.
- (505a–505b) However, we do not have adequate knowledge of what the good is. And without such knowledge we cannot gain any benefit from whatever knowledge we may have of other things.
- (505b–c) Some think the good is pleasure, others that it is knowledge. But to say that it is knowledge amounts to saying that it is knowledge of the good. And it cannot be pleasure since not all pleasures are good.
- (505d–506b) All souls pursue what *really* is the good and not what merely *appears* to be. And although we may have no clear idea of it, we can say that it is that toward which all endeavour is directed. But without knowledge of the good one misses the benefit of other things and so the rulers must know the good if our city is to be perfectly established.

Interpretation

The concept of the good plays a crucial role in the *Republic*, as it is precisely this that the philosophers must gain knowledge of and which enables them to be suitable rulers. By 'the good' Plato means that which we pursue. And by this Plato does not mean the myriad of objects and activities that fuel our everyday desires, but rather the ultimate ends that lie behind these individual activities. For example, Jared might find himself walking down the road with the goal of going to a shop. However, simply arriving at the shop is not Jared's ultimate goal. In this case, he entered the shop to buy a razor. Yet even this is still a means to some other end, namely to shave. Shaving in turn is a means to avoid the itching sometimes created by a beard. Here perhaps we reach the ultimate end or goal – physical comfort. So Jared's walking down the road on that occasion was driven by the fact that he considers physical comfort to be a good. It is claimed that some idea of what is good, or what is in our interest, underpins our every action, even if we do not consciously realise it.

ACTIVITY   Through analysing our everyday activity we can begin to work out what our own conception of the good is. However, according to Plato most of us can only have opinions as to the nature of the good; only true philosophers can gain genuine knowledge. Nevertheless, for each of the activities listed below try to work out what ultimate end or good is being pursued. To help work this out, choose an activity from the list or make one up yourself – let's call this x – and try to complete the following thought: 'I did x in order to do y'. Then take the second part (y) and look for why you did this, i.e. 'I did y in order to do z'. Keep repeating this process until you believe you have reached the ultimate end or good that you were aiming for.

- getting out of bed this morning
- reading this sentence
- wearing smart clothes
- going to work
- buying a packet of crisps
- having children
- cleaning your car
- opening your post

Because we are aiming at some ultimate good or end this confers value on our other activities. In other words many things are good for us in relation to some end or goal we have. For example cars are good for travelling around. So the worth of cars is a function of how much we value travelling. And fresh vegetables are good for us, because they help keep us healthy. So they are good in relation to how much we value our health. However, for Plato, the true good is good simply for its own sake and not in relation to something else. He argues that the ultimate end that we all pursue, that towards which all our actions are aimed, is the Form of the good. The good, Plato suggests, is that which is genuinely in our interest, that which is truly good for us and that which we should pursue. The good is the ultimate object of ethical and metaphysical inquiry. The quest to comprehend the most general principles behind phenomena, i.e. to acquire knowledge of Forms, leads inevitably to the Form of the good. Since the good explains what is *good* in all other things, without knowledge of this Form one cannot fully comprehend ethical (or aesthetic) issues such as what the nature of justice (or beauty) is (505a–b). So if a philosopher hopes to become an effective ruler, he or she must acquire such knowledge (506a–b). The Form of the good thereby takes the place of justice as the goal of the *Republic*'s ethical inquiry.

The claim that things derive their usefulness and value (i.e. what is good in them) from the Form of the good is in line with Plato's general view that things are just, beautiful, etc. in virtue of their relation to justice or beauty as such, that is to the Forms of justice or beauty. The related claim that knowledge is useless without knowledge of the good appears to amount to saying that without such knowledge one cannot expect to be able to plan effectively for the attainment of what is good.

It should be noted that Plato does not draw any firm distinctions between various senses of 'good'. Thus he supposes that what is *morally* good, what is beneficial, useful or profitable *for* someone, what is 'excellent' or good for the kind of thing it is (e.g. when we call someone a 'good' driver), or what is good in virtue of attaining perfection (e.g. the Forms – see below), are all essentially manifestations of the same objective Form of the good.

Just as with the other Forms, a contrast is set up between the good-as-such and relative or qualified goods as encountered in the physical world. Any particular benefit which appears to follow from an action can only be a *relative* or *qualified* good, since it will necessarily be beneficial *for* someone and *in* some respect. And correlatively since the Form of the good is good without qualification, it is good independent of reference to any apparent benefits. Thus what is truly good can be recognised apart from anyone's particular tastes, preferences, and opinions about what is good. Such preferences amount to a partial view of the objective Form of the good. So it is that Socrates can draw a distinction between what *seems* good and what really *is* good.

Note that without an objective and unqualified good there can be no final resolution of conflicts between the interests of different classes, individuals or within one person (e.g. between one's self-interest and one's duty). For Plato, however, all such conflict must be a consequence of the limited apprehension of the good by individuals, that is the confusion of relative goods (e.g. pleasure or knowledge) and *the* good. Thus the lover-of-sights will falsely equate his or her own tastes and pleasures with what is good and in the attempt to satisfy them is liable to come into conflict with other people with incompatible tastes and pleasures. Particular goods, remember, must involve both what is and what is not good, and so inevitably invite conflict. The genuine philosopher will recognise that all such particular goods are pale imitations of the true good, which (if only we recognised it) we would *all* strive for. So by claiming that there is such an objective good, Plato's hope is to escape the possibility of conflicts of interest. The ideal state would reduce conflict to a minimum because its rulers would apprehend what is the greatest good for the community as such.

Evaluation

▶ criticism ◀ At this point however, one may be inclined to object that a thing cannot be termed 'good' *apart* from someone's interest in it. Thus we would normally suppose that what is good or beneficial for one person need not be for someone else. In other words it seems odd to claim that the term 'good' can have an unqualified employment since what is good appears to be inextricably bound up with particular interests. (The same kind of reservation could be made regarding the other Forms, i.e. that they can *only* be meaningfully used in a qualified sense, and consequently that the notion of something which could be just or beautiful *as such* is absurd.) In a similar vein we might argue that the criteria we should use in judging whether some thing or action is good is inescapably dependent on (i.e. qualified by) what *kind* of thing it is. That is to say that what makes a good cup of tea is not the same as what makes a good book, driver or person. (Again one can make the same sort objection with regard to the other Forms.) Thus what relates all good things together is not that they share in one thing.

▶ criticism ◀ Similarly one might consider it strange to say that all human strivings are directed toward *the* good and not toward things in the physical world. Surely an abstract object like 'the good' is not something to spur us into action so much as what benefits us in the physical reality.

▶ criticism ◀ Further, to pick up on a problem already discussed, if the rulers are concerned exclusively with the Form of the good, what motive will they have for seeking to benefit the citizens of a city founded in the physical realm? Plato's response is that once the philosophers see that the good of the city is more akin to *the* good, that is more unqualifiedly good than their own or any one else's interest, they can become motivated to rule. The good of an individual has, in other words, been submerged in *the* good. Nonetheless it remains problematic to understand precisely in what such motivation might consist.

■ The good as a political concept

experimenting with ideas

The importance of *the* good in politics

Today, the question of the ultimate good is rarely discussed explicitly by politicians, although the concept is embedded in nearly all political decisions. Consider the list of possible *ultimate* goods below:

a) personal freedom
b) economic wealth, i.e. gross domestic product (GDP)
c) health and longevity
d) equality
e) knowledge
f) worship of God
g) law and order
h) pleasure
i) advancement of art.

1 Imagine you ruled a small country. Choose three of the possible candidates for *the* good listed above and for each one draft a few laws that you could introduce so as to maximise that good in society. Don't worry if the new law affects other aspects of life or other goods on the list, as for the purpose of the thought experiment they are not *the* good. For example, to maximise **c)** health and longevity, you might introduce a law that completely outlawed all forms of tobacco.

2 For one of *the* goods, revisit the laws and think about whether their introduction would reduce the amount of some of the other goods on the list, in your country. In other words, think about whether pursuing a particular vision of *the* good clashes with other potential visions. For example, introducing a law banning tobacco may maximise **c)** health and longevity; but it would reduce **a)** personal freedom.

3 For the society in which you currently live, what do you think is *the* good, or combination of goods, that the current government is trying to maximise?

Hopefully this activity shows the importance of *the* good as a political concept. All political decisions involve a concept of *the* good, whether implicitly or explicitly. And often politicians are left to juggle different conceptions of *the* good, in an effort to please different groups of people.

In many countries economic growth is one of the key goods being pursued. However, sometimes this can clash with other goods. For example, a city might allow constant night flights transporting produce to and fro in cheap and noisy planes. This sort of activity might improve economic well-being as the produce will be transported cheaply and allow for increased trade. However, the noise of the planes might stop many people sleeping well at night. Superficially at least it seems we have a clash of two different goods, pleasure v. economic well-being. Again, consider the number of bank holidays a country has. In the UK this is eight per year but in many European countries this can be as high as thirteen. Why not have more? One of the major arguments is that it would harm the economic output of the country. Again we seem to have a clash between **b)** and **h)**.

Many liberal democracies assume, unlike Plato, that the question of the ultimate good is best left for each individual to decide. In these countries, governments try to make the laws as liberal as possible so as to permit a wide range of different activities (as long as these activities do not harm others). In this way the individual is free to pursue their own vision of the good. In fact some commentators have gone so far as to say that the good itself simply consists of the pursuit of the good! In other words, a good life is one spent pursuing a vision of what a good life consists of.

Pleasure as the good

Many philosophical theories tell us what the ultimate object of our actions is, that is to say, what we mean by 'good'. Before Plato gives his positive account, he first dismisses two other accounts of what the good is, starting with the idea that the good is pleasure. The view that pleasure or happiness is the ultimate good to which human beings do or should strive is known as HEDONISM, and the best-known hedonist theory is UTILITARIANISM. Utilitarians believe that:

> A good act is one that maximises pleasure/minimises pain.
> A bad act is one that maximises pain/minimises pleasure.

So a utilitarian believes that good acts are those that make the world a happier place overall, whereas bad acts are those that make the world unhappier. Consider this simple example which illustrates the utilitarian position:

> A man, Mr X, goes out one night and mugs Mr Y, stealing £50 from him. Is the world a happier place? Well, Mr X has illegally gained £50 and may derive some happiness from this action, say, 10 units of happiness (an arbitrary measure). However, Mr Y will suffer enormously as a result of this. His suffering may last for a long, long time, so he will lose perhaps 100 units of happiness. His family and friends may also be badly affected and suffer a loss of, say, 80 happiness points. All in all the action has produced +10 new happiness points but caused −180 points worth of suffering. Overall the action has increased the suffering in the world and is thus a bad action.

Socrates dismisses the attempt to equate the good with pleasure, and evil with pain, on the grounds that not all pleasures are good. So hedonists 'find themselves admitting that the same things are both good and bad' (505c), in other words, they believe in a contradiction in terms. No examples are given of bad pleasures, but elsewhere, in the *Gorgias,* Plato argues that some pleasures can lead to bad ends (499) and uses the example of the art of cookery. This art or 'knack' is designed to bring people pleasure, but is not concerned with what is truly good for you. So some foods will taste great and bring short-term pleasure, but they may well not be very good for the health. At the same time, some pains can do good. Medicines may well be very unpleasant to take, and yet they do us good, and so displeasure can be good contrary to the hedonists' claim. Plato may also have in mind that people can gain pleasure from committing morally bad actions, such as stealing. Again, the thought would be that this pleasure is bad, showing that pleasure cannot be equated with the good.

How might a hedonist react to such examples of bad pleasures? If we consider the example of eating tasty but unhealthy foods, a hedonist might respond that the short-term pleasure gained from eating them is offset by the long-term displeasure that results from poor health. So if you want to maximise your pleasure overall, it will be wise not to eat too much unhealthy food, no matter how much pleasure it affords you at the time. This, however, is not to say that eating rich food is a *bad pleasure*, rather it is an action which, on balance, produces more displeasure than pleasure and so, on purely hedonistic principles, may be considered bad. Epicurus, the most important defender of hedonism in the ancient world, argues along these lines in recommending a life of moderation. He believed that to maximise your pleasure over a lifetime, you should live on bread and water and the odd piece of cheese on special occasions.

So what of the pleasure a thief may gain from stealing? Modern hedonists, the utilitarians, would argue in a similar way to Epicurus in pointing out that Plato is not taking into account all the effects of the action. The reason stealing is a bad act is that, if we take everyone into account, not just the thief, it produces much more pain than pleasure overall. It may produce pleasure for one person but it comes at too high a cost in terms of displeasure. So a utilitarian would claim that a *bad pleasure* only appears to be a contradiction. The apparent contradiction occurs because in calling the act *a pleasure* we are only considering the individual's point of view, but in calling the act *bad* we are considering everyone's point of view. It is only by taking these two different perspectives that it is possible to come up with the idea of a *bad pleasure*. It is not really a contradiction at all but merely the same act viewed from different positions. And in calling the act *bad*, we are still confirming that pleasure is the good. So it seems Plato cannot dismiss the idea that pleasure is the good quite so easily.

■ Knowledge as the good

Plato considers the possibility that the good is knowledge. In other words, he is asking whether what we should all ultimately aim for is improving ourselves through education so that we can acquire a deeper grasp of the issues that affect us and gain what we want. But, he asks, what do we ultimately want knowledge *of*? To this he answers 'the good'. The point of acquiring knowledge can only be that we come to know what the good is. So knowledge is not good in itself, rather it is the means by which we come to be acquainted with the good. Plato's idea here seems to be that we need to have knowledge of what is good if we hope to be able to attain it.

The simile of the sun

Having said what the good is not (pleasure and knowledge) Socrates is then asked what it actually is. Socrates says he doesn't know and so elects to use a simile to give an idea of what is not yet clear in his mind. The simile of the sun is the first of three images used to explain both the nature of the Form of the good and its role in the philosophical enterprise. (The other two are the simile of the divided line, 509d–511e, and the simile of the cave, 514a–517c.)

Summary of the argument (506b–509c)

Read 506b–509c

- (506b–507a) But what is the good? Socrates admits he does not know, and he does not want to offer mere opinions. A proper answer is beyond the range of this inquiry. Instead he resolves to discuss a 'child' of the good, that is, something which resembles it, namely the sun.
- (507a–509c) We should recall the distinction between good or beautiful things and the good or beautiful *in itself* (476d–480a). The latter, the Forms, are objects of *thought*, while the former, the particulars, are objects of the *senses* such as sight. Light is essential to the operation of sight, and is provided by the sun. So the sun is both the cause of sight and an object of sight. Now, the sun is the child of the good and is analogous to it. That is to say that the sun

bears the same relation to sight and to visible objects as the good does to thought and to intelligible objects. Just as the sun makes particulars visible, so truth and reality (being) illuminate objects of thought and allow the mind to have knowledge of them. By contrast, when the mind perceives the 'twilight world of change and decay' (508d), namely the physical world in which all things are coming into being and passing away, its intellectual vision is obscured and it can only form opinions. Truth is imparted to objects of knowledge, and the power of knowing is imparted to the knower by the Form of the good. So while truth and knowledge are good, they are distinct from *the* good, just as sight and light are (in some sense) 'sunlike', but are distinct from the sun. Finally, the sun is the source not only of physical objects' visibility, but also of their powers of generation, growth and nourishment, while not itself being such a power. And, equivalently, the good is the cause not simply of objects of knowledge being knowable, but also of their capacity to *be*, while it is not itself being (or reality), since it transcends it.

Interpretation

There are four main points of the analogy.

1 The good is responsible for the possession of 'truth' by things that are known, i.e. Forms (507b), and for our knowledge of them; just as the sun is responsible for the colours possessed by visible objects and for our ability to see them (508d–e).

The good causes things to possess truth and causes our knowledge of them, according to Plato, because to have knowledge of something is to know that it bears a certain relation to the good. So what is this relation and why is it required for knowledge? Perhaps Plato's thought is that to know a Form involves knowing that it is a good thing, since all Forms, insofar as they are unqualifiedly what they are, are the best (i.e. *most good*) examples of that quality. They are, after all, perfect, or non-defective specimens. So, on this interpretation, the Form of justice would be good, since it is *perfectly* just, while particulars are inferior or 'less good' examples. Particular actions will be 'better' in respect of justice the more they approximate to justice-as-such, i.e. to the best version of justice. So to know the Form of justice involves knowledge of what a *good* specimen of justice is, and so involves knowledge of the good.

In viewing Plato's meaning in this way it is helpful to recognise that Plato sees the ideas of perfection, unity and stability as closely related to that of goodness. For example, the ideal city is good because it has no internal conflicts, which is to say that it is unified and one. This also means it is liable to last, since, for Plato, decadence is the consequence of internal strife and division. So imperfection is associated with change and decay within the physical world, but objects which are perfect, namely the Forms, must endure eternally. This means that knowledge of a particular Form must involve understanding what it is to be a perfect version of that Form.

However, this doesn't really explain why we need to know what the good is in order properly to have knowledge of the other Forms. One way to make sense of this claim is to suppose Plato is saying we can derive knowledge of all the other Forms from knowledge of the Form of the good. This is because, on Plato's way of thinking, knowing the ultimate aim or purpose of anything constitutes understanding that thing. For example, in order properly to know what a bed is, I need to know what it is for or, in other words, what it is that makes it a good bed. Understanding the function of something is necessary for being able to judge how well it performs its function, or how far it succeeds in fulfilling its role as that thing. So knowing what a bed is good for is to know what a bed is. This would mean that knowing the Form of the bed would be possible only if we had a clear understanding of what makes it a good bed. To see how this might work, let's suppose that the good was pleasure and that pleasure is the only true aim worth pursuing. If this were the case then the perfect bed would be that which brings the most pleasure and so working out what such a bed would be becomes a relatively straightforward matter. This shows that once the good is known then knowledge of all the other Forms can be derived in relation to it. In this sense, then, the Form of the good allows for the knowledge of the other Forms.

What these claims amount to is that true knowledge is not a simple matter of knowing what something *is*, but what it *ought* to be: that is to say, what it is *good* for. For to have knowledge of something is to recognise what its *purpose* is, i.e. that for the sake of which it is what it is. This is because, for Plato, the account or explanation (*logos*) of the ultimate nature of beauty or justice will inevitably be teleological in nature. Put another way this means that knowing that the Forms are perfect exemplars of their kind is of little use unless one is able to deploy that knowledge to some end, and this ultimately involves acquiring knowledge of the good.

2   The good is the cause of the being (existence) of
    intelligible objects, in the same way as the sun is the cause
    of the generation and growth of visible objects (509b). In
    other words, just as the sun sustains living things in the
    physical realm, so too the Form of the good gives being to
    the Forms.

**more
difficult**

What does it mean to give being to the other Forms? One
way to understand Plato's meaning is to consider that if a
Form is unqualifiedly such-and-such (e.g. beautiful), and to
that extent good, then its *being*, i.e. what it essentially *is*,
involves the good. The Forms are what they are because they
are good and, in a sense, then, their being can be thought to
be possible *because of* the Form of the good. So since we
deploy the Form of the good to discover the other Forms, it
is through them that their nature is determined. This means it
is the good which makes them what they are, and this may be
what Plato has in mind in saying that the good gives them
their being.

3   The good is said to be beyond being or reality in 'dignity
    and power' in the same way as the sun is beyond the
    processes of generation that it engenders (509b).

The principal idea here is that the Form of the good is the
ultimate object of inquiry and superior to the other Forms in
terms of reality and perfection. This is not, however, to say
that the good transcends being and lies beyond the realm of
the other Forms, but rather that it is the most real and perfect
because it is what sustains the being of the other Forms and
that which confers upon them their perfection and reality.

Note also that Plato wants here to emphasise that although
the Form of the good causes the other Forms to *be*, this
doesn't mean that it *is* being-as-such. In other words, the
good is not the Form of being in which the other Forms
partake in order to be. Plato makes the point because
normally that which gives things some property is the Form
of that property.

4   The sun doesn't just illuminate other objects and make
    them visible, but also is visible itself, and in the same way
    the good doesn't just make other Forms knowable, but can
    itself be an object of knowledge (508b–c).

Here Socrates is saying that although he does not yet know
what it is, the good is knowable. The search for a definition
of its essence may be difficult, but, as with the other Forms, it
is not in vain. And its discovery is the ultimate goal of
philosophy.

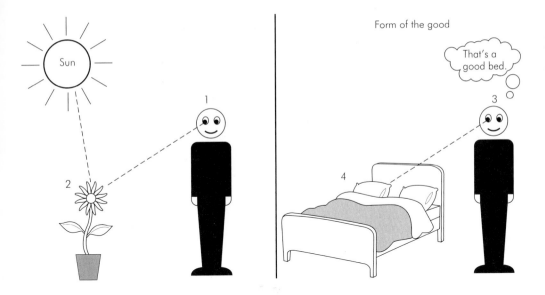

Figure 6.1 *The simile of the sun*
The sun enables sight (1) and also sustains the growth of living things (2), just as the Form of the good enables us to know the Forms (3) and sustains the being of the Forms (4)

Evaluation

While suggestive, what is frustrating about the simile of the sun is that ultimately it tells us very little about what the good actually is. All Socrates is able to convey is the key role it plays within the wider theory of Forms and its importance as the ultimate goal of philosophical inquiry. So what are we to make of the role he has painted for the Form of the good?

One difficulty is making sense of the idea that the Form of the good can allow for the being of the other Forms. However, so far we have only looked at the standard interpretation of Plato's theory of Forms. There is another interpretation of the theory that makes the simile of the sun more intelligible. The standard version suggests that the Forms actually exist in another realm and that their existence is independent of human minds. The alternative 'secular' interpretation of the theory of Forms suggests that Plato did not consider the Forms to exist in another realm, but saw them rather as ideal concepts in the mind. On this second view, the existence of other Forms is a possible because of the good in the same way as knowledge of them is possible because of the good, as we saw above. However, critics of this secular interpretation would claim that it cannot be what Plato intended as Plato often talks of two distinct realms, of how the Forms exist independently from humans. Defenders of the interpretation would reply that the occasional suggestion of two realms is simply a simile to show the distinctness of the mental from the physical.

Through the simile of the sun Socrates has developed his picture of the nature of the objects of knowledge. The thrust of his argument has been to show that the Form of the good is the supreme reality and the source of the reality of all the Forms. It is by means of the Form of the good that knowledge of the other Forms is possible and so the quest for knowledge of the good is the ultimate goal of the philosopher. He now turns to some other similes which attempt to further elucidate his rather elusive idea.

Key points: Chapter 6

What you need to know about the **simile of the sun**:

1 The most important subject for a philosopher to study is the Form of the good.
2 The good represents that which we all strive for, but most people will only have an opinion as to what this should be.
3 Socrates claims that the good is not pleasure, nor is it knowledge. In denying the good as pleasure Plato is going against the later philosophy of utilitarianism.
4 The Form of the good enables all other knowledge to be possible and also enables the other Forms to exist. This point is made through the simile of the sun.

7

The simile of the line

Introduction

After the simile of the sun the audience is still not clear as to the nature of the good, so Socrates offers the simile of the line to aid their understanding. This chapter examines this simile, which explores further the relationship between the two realms of reality and offers a more detailed account of Plato's theory of knowledge.

The simile of the divided line

Summary of the argument (509d–511e)

Read 509d–511e

- (509d–510b) We have divided things into the realm of the visible and the realm of the intelligible. These two realms can be represented on a vertical line divided into two sections, each of which can be further subdivided to make four subsections in all (see Figure 7.1). Each subsection represents a level of clarity. The first within the visible realm (D) contains 'images' (*eikones*), i.e. 'shadows' or 'reflections'. The second (C) contains the objects which produce these images, such as living things or artefacts. The relation between the two, namely of image to original, or copy to pattern, is the same as that of opinion to knowledge.
- (510b–511c) The upper part of the line represents the intelligible realm. In the first section (B) the mind uses things in level C (namely, the originals of 'images') in turn as images, and also uses HYPOTHESES or assumptions. For example, students of geometry, arithmetic and the other sciences use visible figures as images or illustrations of the original objects of their investigations, which can only be apprehended by reason. And they use hypotheses which they regard as known and proceed to their conclusions. Consequently they do not proceed to a first principle. In the highest subsection (A) the mind contemplates Forms alone. This is the study of the science of *dialectic*, which proceeds without the use of images and hypotheses to ascend to a first principle that is not hypothetical.

Having grasped the principle the student of dialectic descends to conclusions. The whole procedure has nothing to do with the sensible world but deals exclusively with Forms. The crucial thing is to distinguish between the science of dialectic and other procedures.

■ (511c–e) Glaucon summarises the simile, and Socrates explains that there are four states of mind corresponding to the four sections of the line, namely (A) dialectic (*noesis*), (B) mathematical reasoning (*dianoia*), (C) belief (*pistis*), (D) illusion (*eikasia*). *Pistis* and *eikasia* are subdivisions of opinion (*doxa*); and *noesis* and *eikasia* are subdivisions of knowledge (*episteme*).

Interpretation

Plato asks us to imagine a line divided into two unequal parts. And each of these parts is to be further divided in two in the same ratio. These confusing instructions produce a line with four distinct sections. These four sections will come to represent four different states of knowledge (epistemic states) A, B, C and D. There are also four different types of object that correspond to these four states.

The simile is a rough sketch which although suggestive of much does not explore the ideas it raises in any detail. The

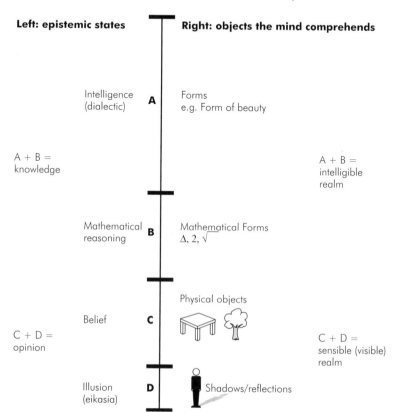

■ **Figure 7.1 Plato asks us to imagine a line divided into four sections, representing on the one hand four different epistemic states of mind and on the other four categories of object the mind deals with**

Left: epistemic states

Right: objects the mind comprehends

Intelligence (dialectic) **A** — Forms e.g. Form of beauty

A + B = knowledge

A + B = intelligible realm

Mathematical reasoning **B** — Mathematical Forms Δ, 2, √

Physical objects

Belief **C**

C + D = opinion

C + D = sensible (visible) realm

Illusion (eikasia) **D** — Shadows/reflections

main aim is to emphasise the distinction between the sensible (visible) and intelligible, or between what is apparent (namely 'images') and what is real (the original objects). The distinction is made in terms of the different ways in which we gain an understanding of the two realms.

The opposite of perfect knowledge is complete ignorance, which would presumably sit beneath the bottom of the line. Just above complete ignorance and rising up to full knowledge lie various stages of clarity. Plato in the simile of the line tries to explain what these increasing states of clarity are. He suggests there are four stages of knowledge and tries to represent them as increasingly large segments on a line, culminating in the largest representing perfect knowledge. The lowest of the states – situated at the bottom of the line – is the state of *eikasia* (roughly translating as illusion).

■ The four stages of knowledge

D   Illusion (*eikasia*)

Plato asks us to imagine the sort of knowledge that could be gained from looking at shadows of things, or by looking at rippled reflections. He calls the state of mind when we contemplate such things *eikasia* (illusion). Imagine looking at the shadow of a tree; you may be able to glean some information, perhaps even tell which type of tree it is, but you would have no idea of the true shape or colours. Such a state would be better than complete ignorance but falls far short of true knowledge. This is the state of *eikasia*, better than ignorance, but not much. Later Plato also classes observing art as an example of *eikasia*, the idea being that art is an indirect 'reflection' of the world through an artist's mind. In making this claim Plato is suggesting that art cannot lead us to the truth about reality. One difficulty of interpretation of this stage of knowledge is that it is not really clear what the mental state of *eikasia* is. It is plausible to regard belief and knowledge are different mental states as it feels quite different to know something for certain (for example, that water makes paper wet), than it does merely to believe something (for example, that England will win the next world cup). However, on a psychological level looking at shadows doesn't really produce a feeling that is radically different from just looking at general objects, at least not a difference that is easy to diagnose.

C   Belief

The next state, slightly clearer than *eikasia*, is that of belief. This occurs when we behold the physical objects around us – trees, tables, rivers and so on; in other words, all the objects in the sensible world. Plato is here making the now familiar point that the senses alone cannot yield genuine knowledge; they can only give us opinions about the world of change and decay. We must remember that, for Plato, true knowledge does not include grasp of such facts as 'the table in my lounge is brown' since knowledge concerns universal and necessary truths, truths which remain true in all time and all places. These truths will not be gained by the senses alone according to Plato; the senses can only reveal the world of change, not the eternal world of truths.

Consider the example of a table to see what Plato has in mind. By using your senses you may have a theory as to what makes a good table, what the perfect table would be like. But this would only ever be a belief, even if it were the correct belief. Only if you knew the Form of the good would you then be able to truly *know* what the perfect table was like (that which brought about the most good). The same can be said for beauty: using your eyes you could run around, like the sight lovers, and behold many paintings and objects of art; you might draw your own conclusions as to what is and is not beautiful. However, this again would only be a belief. Only if you apprehended the Form of beauty would you truly know what is and is not beautiful. So the world around us cannot yield knowledge. This will only come when we apprehend the Forms.

D and C, in terms of objects, together comprise the physical, sensible world. In terms of mental states, they collectively represent *doxa*, which roughly translates as opinion.

B Mathematical reasoning

The next highest epistemic state is that of mathematical reasoning, which occurs when our mind contemplates mathematical concepts and objects like numbers, triangles, straight lines, etc. When our mind leaves behind the particular shapes and groups of objects in this world and contemplates ideal shapes and numbers, we enter this new higher state of knowledge. In this state, by using reason, we are able to establish the eternal truths of mathematics. Plato, along with many philosophers since, is very impressed with the way that mathematical truths can be gained with absolute certainty. These are truths established by the mind and which then apply in all cases throughout the world. Our minds are somehow grasping truths that are beyond the senses, truths of another purer realm. Plato sees this as the model for all knowledge. However, he does not consider mathematical reasoning to be the highest Form of knowledge. The reason for this seems two-fold. Firstly Plato seems to suggest that, because geometry and maths start with observations of the physical world and how it behaves, they are somehow not fully pure. Secondly geometry uses assumptions that are themselves not proven, for example that two parallel lines never meet, or that a straight line is the shortest distance between two points. From these assumptions, or axioms as they are sometimes called, a host of truths about triangles and other shapes can be proven. But assumptions, however obvious they may appear, are still needed in the first place. Plato seems to be treating mathematical concepts as a sort of 'mini-Forms', perhaps Forms that at least on some level are accessible to most people. However, mathematical Forms are derived from the sensible world whereas the other Forms will be derived from the first principle, presumably the Form of the good.

A   Intelligence (dialectic)

The highest form of knowledge is reserved for when our minds contemplate the pure Forms. Plato envisions that just as we grasp the concept of a number so too can we grasp concepts such as 'beauty' or 'justice'. This will be achieved through reasoning using the method known as dialectic. Plato is not very clear about exactly how this will come about but suggests that this can be done using pure reason, and '*involves nothing in the sensible world*'. Using the dialectic the philosopher is somehow able to reach a first principle, which is not based on an assumption, and from this first principle is able to work out subsequent truths. As this follows on from the simile of the sun, the first principle would presumably be an understanding of the Form of the good. Perhaps it is a definition or set of propositions about the good.

An interesting parallel may be drawn here with the quest in modern physics whereby scientists pursue a single basic principle that can unite all the different branches of physics. From this basic principle or idea the rest of science could then be derived (in theory). However, the difference between the quest in modern science and Plato's vision is that scientific theories, however abstract and mathematical they may appear, are based on observations and data about the sensible world.

A and B, in terms of objects, represent the intelligible realm. In terms of mental states, they represent knowledge.

The simile of the divided line

Interpretation and evaluation

■ Left and right of the line

When considering the line it is important to remember that the line represents two different things at the same time. On the one hand it represents four different mental states culminating in knowledge. On the other hand it represents the four different kinds of objects that correspond to each state – i.e. shadows, physical objects, mathematical objects and Forms. It is important to remember that for Plato, and for the Greeks, each mental state or faculty had to have a corresponding class of objects that it deals with. Knowledge is thus always knowledge *of* something (knowledge by acquaintance) rather than knowledge *that* ... (propositional knowledge). So in defining the four different epistemic states Plato has to define the four different types of object they correspond to.

▶ criticism ◀ Distinguishing knowledge from opinion on the basis of the different kinds of objects the mind deals with is an approach that may be criticised. Certainly in everyday life we tend to distinguish the two in terms of the way they grasp something, rather than the thing they grasp. So we tend to think that knowledge and belief can be about the same kinds of object. Knowledge is just a special kind of belief, a belief with very strong evidence. For example, you might *believe* there is a dog outside your house, on the basis of some faint noises you hear. However, if you popped your head outside the window and saw a little lost dog outside your house, you might now want to claim that you *knew* this for sure. So here it is possible to have knowledge or belief about the same kinds of thing, i.e. the whereabouts of the dog, belief and knowledge being separated by degrees of evidence.

Having said this, it is nonetheless true that certain areas of thought such as morality and musical taste are only capable of yielding beliefs or opinions. So it is still possible in some instances to distinguish what can be known from what can only be believed on the basis of the type of object considered. Oddly though, such people would claim that it is impossible to know about musical taste or morality as there is no corresponding truth to such matters; which is exactly the opposite of Plato's philosophy. For Plato it is precisely the areas of morality and taste that can be known.

Up and down the line

One of the main aims of the simile is to emphasise the distinction between the sensible realm and intelligible realm, or between what is apparent (namely 'images') and what is real (the original objects). However, Plato does not draw a simple parallel but one continuous line. In so doing he suggests that the bottom section is not simply an analogy for the top. Rather each segment represents a degree of understanding or clarity along which one can progress from the visible world to that of the Forms. Clarity increases as one becomes acquainted with what is closer to the 'original'. Thus perceiving objects is an improvement on perceiving mere reflections in the visible realm. And mathematical objects are in turn more original than sensible ones. The latter are deployed as 'images' in order for the mind to reason on the original mathematical objects, much as images might be deployed to acquire an understanding of physical objects. Finally mathematics relates to dialectic in the same manner, namely as image to original; although it is not entirely clear what this means. We have in other words a description of a journey, the journey of the philosopher, from a state of illusion and concern with 'images' in the sensible realm, through to direct acquaintance in the intelligible realm with the ultimate objects of knowledge. In this way the line sketches the path that the rulers' education takes through a variety of sciences toward dialectic and culminating in knowledge of the good (531d–534d).

The line as a simile

Most of Plato's similes are fairly colourful, often involving scenarios and stories, but the line has none of these characteristics, and is not a very interesting image at all. It appears to function more as a diagram, outlining various aspects of Plato's theory of knowledge, rather than as a simile.

What are we to make of the specific ratios in the line? (The line is divided unequally in two and then each half is divided unequally in the same ratio.) Plato is not very clear on this. One obvious point is that by making the sections increase in size Plato is referring to the increasing clarity of knowledge that accompanies the move from using the senses alone to using reason. But it seems likely that there is another meaning, particularly as Plato asks us to imagine a line divided in two and then divided each segment again in the same ratio. Why should the ratio be the same again?

■ Figure 7.2
As shadows are to
objects, so the
sensible world is to
the intelligible world

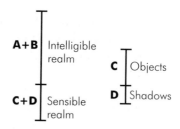

Plato could be suggesting that the intelligible world (A + B) is much clearer than the sensible world (C + D) much in the way that objects (C) are much clearer than their shadows (D). In other words the whole world of the senses is itself like a shadow compared to the intelligible world. Plato is comparing the relationship of C to D to that of AB to CD. This interpretation marries well with the next simile, that of the cave, where a comparison is first made between shadows and the objects that cast the shadows, then later between the objects within the cave and the real objects outside, the former being a pale imitation of the latter. This would make the purpose of the line very similar to that of the sun. Plato is simply drawing a parallel between the visible and intelligible to help us understand the latter. Like the simile of the sun, the visible realm is operating as an 'image' or reflection of the intelligible.

This interpretation is further strengthened by the following consideration. What are we to make of the concept of illusion (*eikasia*)? As mentioned previously, the Greeks believed that each different mental faculty was defined by the types of object that the faculty deals with. For example, vision and hearing are different faculties, and correspondingly they deal with different types of object, i.e. colours and sounds. This belief is present throughout the simile of the line. Here Plato describes four mental faculties (*eikasia*, belief, reasoning, intelligence) and he does so by describing the four different types of object (shadows, physical objects, mathematical objects, Forms) that each deals with. Each faculty is defined by the class of objects it deals with. The faculty of *eikasia* is quite strange in as much as we are not usually aware of being in a particular mental state when observing shadows and the like; it doesn't feel much different to just observing objects in general, and hardly seems worthy of a special name. Also the class of objects that *eikasia* deals with, shadows and reflections, does not really form a natural class of objects. Perhaps section D is really present merely to complete the notion of a progression from virtual ignorance to full knowledge and to allow for the comparison outlined in the diagram above.

▶ criticism ◀ By specifying the ratios so clearly in the simile Plato can also be interpreted as claiming that B is to A as D is to C: that numbers and geometrical shapes are to Forms as shadows are to their objects. This does not really seem to make much sense, however. It's hard to understand in what sense numbers are the shadows of Forms. Mathematics seems to be a clear and precise field. Indeed it's hard to see how it could be any more clear or precise. Perhaps Plato is making the point that a shadow relies on something else, namely an object, to exist and, reasoning about shapes, maths also relies on something else, namely the world and the use of assumptions. However, it is far from clear that this is the point being made.

Perhaps the main point in separating A from B, in making two orders within the intelligible realm, is to distinguish between the kind of knowledge we can have with, as opposed to without, knowledge of the good. Beliefs about objects and shadows, and knowledge of maths and shapes, are also possible without knowledge of the good. However, true intelligence requires knowledge of the good, and only with knowledge of the good can we use our knowledge to achieve anything worthwhile.

Rationalism

The simile of the line also emphasises the rationalist element in Plato's philosophy. RATIONALISM is the philosophical approach that treats reason as the important source of knowledge (empiricism suggests it is the senses, and mysticism suggests it is a higher source – perhaps divine revelation – see page 167 for more details). We can see in the line that Plato is making a clear distinction between knowledge and opinion and at the same time between the intelligible and the visible/sensible world. The point that the visible world can only ever yield opinions, not knowledge, is a clear statement of his rationalist convictions. However, most philosophers nowadays regard reason as incapable of providing any new knowledge or information about the world. Indeed, the remarkable success of the sciences in modern times would have been impossible without experimentation, i.e. observation using the senses.

Key points: Chapter 7

What you need to know about the **simile of the line**:

1 Socrates represents four different epistemic states as segments on a divided line. These states are *eikasia* (illusion), belief, reasoning and intelligence. The first two represent opinion; the latter two represent knowledge.

2 On the same line Socrates outlines four different classes of objects: shadows, physical objects, mathematical objects and Forms. The four sets of objects correspond to the four epistemic states outlined in **1**.

3 The simile of the line reveals Plato's theory of knowledge, which claims that knowledge can only be gained through grasping the Forms and denies the possibility of gaining knowledge through the senses.

4 As a simile it is not entirely clear what is represented by the positioning of the divisions on the line.

8

The simile of the cave

Introduction

Immediately after the simile of the line, Plato proceeds with yet another simile, that of the cave. This is perhaps the most famous section in all of Plato's writings and forms the main focus of this chapter. The simile compares the human condition of understanding to the life of some prisoners in a cave, and offers the reader a more poetic account of Plato's theory of knowledge than that provided in the previous simile of the line.

This chapter contains the following main sections:

- The simile of the cave
- Use of simile in the *Republic* – extended analysis
- Returning to the cave
- Plato's theory of knowledge 2 – extended analysis.

The simile of the cave

Summary of the argument (514a–517c)

Read 514a–517c

- (514a–515c) Ordinary people are likened to prisoners chained in a cave so that they can only look toward a wall opposite the entrance. Onto this wall shadows are cast by puppets and other artefacts which are carried in front of a fire behind them. The prisoners can only ever see these shadows, and consequently believe them to be real objects. Further, because there is an echo, they also take the voices of the people passing to be coming from the shadows.
- (515c–517a) If a prisoner were released and forced to turn and walk toward the fire he would be too dazed properly to see the shapes whose shadows he had been watching. If asked to compare the objects with the shadows he would inevitably take the latter to be truer since they were clearer to him. It would be more difficult still for someone led out of the cave to see in the sunlight. At first he would be unable to look at real things directly and would have to look at their shadows and reflections. But later he would be able to look at the things themselves, and finally he would be able to look at the sun. Once he saw the sun he would

become aware that it controls everything in the visible realm and is the source of all those things he used to see in the cave. He would much prefer this state to being in the cave; and if he went back down again his sight would at first be poor in the darkness, and his fellows would claim that his sight has been ruined by leaving the cave.

■ (517b–c) The simile of the cave is to be fitted in with what has gone before (namely, the other two similes). The visible world corresponds to the cave, and the light of the fire to the power of the sun. The ascent from the cave to seeing things outside represents the journey of the soul to the intelligible realm. The sun represents the Form of the good which is perceived last. It is the cause of all things that are right and beautiful, and must be seen by anyone who is to be able to act rationally.

ACTIVITY   Read and draw the initial scenario presented in the simile of the cave.

Interpretation

Plato invites us to imagine the following scenario. Some people have been tied against a wall nearly all their lives in virtual darkness; they stare at a wall opposite. Behind and above them is a fire; in front of this, people walk about behind a screen holding up objects. Because of the fire burning behind, these shapes cast shadows on the wall in front of the prisoners. These shadows are all that the prisoners can see. Plato suggests that, because this is all they have been exposed to during their whole lives, the prisoners will naturally assume that this shadow display is the only reality that exists. Further, we are asked to imagine that one of the prisoners is somehow freed from his shackles and clambers up towards the fire behind. At first his eyes will struggle but eventually he will see the puppets and other objects that cause the shadows. Immediately, his entire world view will be shattered; now he sees what reality is. But this is not all we are to imagine: this prisoner slowly works his way up and out of the cave to the light beyond. When he goes outside his eyes will initially be blinded. At first he will look at the shadows on the ground; then all the glorious objects around him, their colours and shapes; then the stars and moon; finally he will see the sun in its splendid glory. Only then can he finally grasp true reality. Imagine then that this freed prisoner returns to the cave to tell his fellows about the wonderful reality outside, and how their shadow world is but a pale imitation. These other prisoners will naturally be very hostile towards him, and not believe a word he says, unable to imagine a reality beyond their own.

What does this all mean? The prisoners represent all of mankind, fixated by their belief that the visible world is all that exists, happy that their world view represents the only truth. The freed prisoner represents the philosopher who has apprehended the intelligible, has grasped the true Forms of which the objects around us are but pale imitations. Naturally, society is hostile to this man, thinking he is a babbling fool. The simile in many ways reflects the treatment dished out to Socrates by Athenian society.

The simile is a poetic representation of Plato's two-world view and his theory of knowledge. However, does it add to our understanding of Plato's theory of knowledge? Also, does it present a picture consistent with the similes of the line and the sun?

Evaluation

■ Mapping the cave onto the line

Through the simile of the cave Plato provides a more vivid picture of the journey of his philosophers to knowledge and of their subsequent return to the ordinary world where they will govern. Philosophy is presented as a liberating and enlightening experience; while by contrast the ordinary condition of mankind is one of intellectual imprisonment.

Socrates tells us that the simile of the cave should be 'fitted together', or 'connected' with what has gone before, namely the similes of the sun and the line. We are told that the cave and fire represent the visible world, and the ascent represents the progress of the mind into the intelligible realm.

As in the simile of the line, within the cave there is a progression from images to originals. So we might expect to be able to map the various cognitive states described in the line with the various stages of the character's journey from the cave.

ACTIVITY Recall the four subsections A, B, C, D of the line (see page 144 above).

1 Which features/stages of the cave might represent the different subsections of the line?
2 What might the sun represent?

■ Problems with mapping the cave on to the line

The most common way of matching up the two similes is as follows: the prisoners' condition of watching the wall represents subsection D on the line; turning to the fire and looking at the shapes represents C; climbing to the outside and looking at reflections outside represents B; and seeing real things represents A. Seeing the sun represents attaining knowledge of the good.

We can see that initially the line seems to map quite well against the simile of the cave. In the line there are two distinct realms: the sensible realm and the intelligible realm. In the simile of the cave there are also two distinct realms: the dark world inside the cave and the bright world outside. There are two different stages within each of the realms in the line and there are different journey stages both inside and outside of the cave. It appears that the cave is simply a more picturesque version of the simile of the line.

▶ criticism ◀ However, this superficial correspondence may be misleadingly simple. In the simile of the line, what are we to assume is the normal mental state of a human? Presumably it is C (belief) – beholding the objects around us. But what does the cave suggest is the normal condition of mankind? It surely suggests that it is D – *eikasia* (illusion) – beholding shadows and reflections. There is an inconsistency here. Which is Plato's real view? Which state of ignorance does Plato believe humankind inhabits? It seems hard to believe that we are in a permanent state of *eikasia*, for surely most of the time we don't look at shadows but rather at the objects that cause them. However, if we expanded the concept of *eikasia* to include things other than just shadows and reflections, then perhaps the picture put forward by the cave is a more accurate account of the human condition. Later in the book Plato suggests that beholding art also produces *eikasia*. He argues that a drawing, sculpture or poem is a kind of *reflection* of reality through the artist's mind. This would bring more elements into the state of *eikasia* and make the account of the human condition put forward by the cave more convincing. Even with this inclusion though, it does not seem reasonable to claim that humans mainly use reflections, shadows and art to forge their opinions of the world.

However, some commentators suggest that we should go farther still. They suggest that all ideas gained from second-hand information, from books or through others, also produce *eikasia*. Such information, it is argued, is also like a reflection of reality through the mind of another. If this sounds reasonable then Plato's assertion (in the cave) that we all live in a state of illusion (*eikasia*) is more plausible because most of our knowledge, our construction of the past, our beliefs about reality have come through others, through books, the media, schools, etc.

ACTIVITY   Second-hand knowledge

Much of your knowledge will have come from second-hand sources, i.e. from other people, books, newspapers, TV, the Internet or radio. Without these sources, what would you know about:

■ the history of the world?
■ the theory of evolution?
■ geography?
■ world news?

How much about the world have you actually derived purely by yourself from either your senses or your own reasoning?

From the activity above, you will probably have realised that most of your knowledge comes from second-hand sources. If we include this 'reflected' knowledge in the category of *eikasia* then the epistemic condition of man, as portrayed in the cave, seems to be more accurate.

In fact some have suggested that, in modern times, it has become an increasingly accurate account of the human condition. Recently, the simile of the cave has been re-interpreted in light of the rise of the modern media. Plato's suggestion that our view of reality comes from watching two-dimensional images projected on to a wall has a whole new resonance in the age of television. It is suggested that most people's world view has been constructed around the words and images seen on television and newspapers. Media executives decide what stories count as newsworthy, which events are more important than others and which slant to put on the news. In doing so a 'world view' emerges from the media. Commentators such as Noam Chomsky suggest that this world view is manipulated by those in power to perpetuate the status quo and the interests of powerful elites.

Such a view maps very easily onto the simile of the cave. The masses are the prisoners chained to the wall watching the televisions. Some are freed and are able to see the strange puppeteers constructing the shadows; this would relate to the media moguls/politicians who control the images and words we are exposed to. True knowledge emerges when we step outside the 'cave' and view the world beyond the reach of the media manipulators. How far you could take this sort of analysis, however, is debatable, after all, mass media did not exist in Plato's day so could not have been a target of the cave simile.

Use of simile in the *Republic* – extended analysis

We must remember that the sun, the line and the cave are similes and we should not expect to find perfectly fitting accounts of knowledge in each of them. The difficulty with reconciling the similes suggests they are only intended to illustrate the general direction of the ascent of the soul, rather than to provide a detailed account. Indeed part of the point of the similes has been to tell us to be wary of illustration and image. Knowledge has to do with contemplation of the originals. The lesson therefore may be that we should use these images as tools to progress beyond and towards the true object of Plato's analysis. For concentrating on the images and attempting to work them out in detail involves losing sight of the original.

However, we cannot ignore the similes: if the similes were removed, without them the *Republic* would be incomparably poorer as both literature and philosophy. And as Plato never gave a straightforward account of the theory of Forms, we are left to try to construct the theory largely from the similes in the *Republic* and elsewhere. It is worth briefly thinking about the role of simile in argument.

A simile is a figure of speech in which objects or features of the world are compared to others. Usually, similes are marked by use of the words *as* or *like*. For example 'their relationship felt as comfortable as an old shoe'. Similes are classed as part of metaphorical language – language that is not literally true but adds to our understanding or enjoyment of the world. For example 'The sun has got his hat on' is not literally true but implies that the sun is dazzling and radiant and much like someone dressed in their best clothes (including their hat).

Similes can be used poetically to stress a point or to make us think differently about an object. However, they can also be a means of argument, something we know Plato is fond of. Using a simile as part of an argument would generally be classed as an example of argument by analogy.

This brief analysis has already generated three terms: metaphor, simile and analogy. These terms are often used fairly interchangeably so in different books you may read about the *metaphor* of the cave, the *simile* of the cave or the *analogy* of the cave. On one level it's not really important how we describe the cave, the line, etc. 'Analogy' is probably the most philosophically accurate as it describes the kind of argument Plato is presenting; however, the term 'simile' is more widely used, which is why we have adopted it throughout this book.

How are we to read similes?

When a poet compares his love to a red, red rose there will be certain features of the rose that he thinks also apply to his love: perhaps the fragrance, beauty, the fact that it is natural, that it blooms, perhaps also that it is thorny. Of course, there will be other features in any simile that the author did not intend to select as relevant to the topic, such as the fact that roses grow well in manure and are prone to greenfly.

In a poetic context the author might not be specific about which features of the rose are to apply to his love. However, when used as an argument the proponent is claiming that specific features of the object in the simile are like specific feature of the topic under discussion. Reading the simile is being able to pick out the relevant features and see if they shed any new light on the topic in question.

For example a Prime Minister might want to raise taxes to slow down the growth of the economy and so prevent inflation. This might not be popular with the public. The Prime Minister might argue that the economy is like a sickly child who needs some unpleasant medicine. The Prime Minister is claiming that there are features of giving medicine to a child, a short-term unpleasant measure for a long-term benefit, that apply to the raising of taxes to benefit the economy.

In this case the use of the analogy might also serve as an explanation for people who might not understand how the economy works. The analogy uses a feature of the world that people may know something about to explain a feature that they may not. However, the Prime Minister might want to claim more than a mere means of explanation; he might believe that in certain regards the treatment of the child and the economy are genuinely similar.

Is argument from analogy a legitimate form of argument?

First we should note that argument from analogy can be highly effective. Analogies are often used by politicians to get their messages across and are extensively used by the advertising industry. Many advertisements compare features of a different and often respected item with the product they are trying to sell. For example the handling of a car might be compared to the movements of a gazelle, or the protective power of toothpaste compared to the protection offered in battle by a shield. However, many forms of argument are effective but not legitimate. Such methods were of course taught by the sophists and were strongly rejected by Socrates and Plato who championed the cause of reason.

So is arguing by analogy a valid use of reason or simply a logically invalid use of rhetoric?

Much will depend on whether the features of the object in the simile are relevant or suitably similar to the features of the object you are trying to shed light on. For example, in the argument presented above by the Prime Minister it might well be countered that the raising of taxes takes place over a much longer period than simply taking a spoonful of medicine – so is not analogous. Also the economy is ever-changing and is affected by other dominant economies in the world; unlike the child's body, there is no easy conception of normality for the economy to return to. This analogy may be useful in helping those who did not understand the rationale for the tax rise to get a simple idea of the principle, but the analogy does not shed any new light on the nature of the economy. It may be a persuasive tool to get voters on board, but it would not count as a legitimate rationale if a tax increase were based purely on the analogy alone.

However, there are many cases where use of analogy does help to shed new light on an area of the world. For example, analogy is used a lot in science, often just for explanation but analogies can also turn into fully fledged theories. In terms of explanation, think of the pictorial model of an atom used in teaching science. Atoms are invisible to the eye, so the question of what they 'look' like is somewhat problematic. We choose to represent the atom as a picture that resembles how we might represent the solar system: a central cluster of balls with much smaller balls whizzing around. We are comparing something we cannot see with something that we are familiar with, i.e. ball-like objects. Of course the 'truth' of this analogy is a different matter – whether electrons are situated in space or not is a complex question – but the model does serve to help us understand a little better.

Maps work in a similar way. However, in this case we want the analogy to be 'true'. In the real world, objects have spatial relations to one another: for example, a tree may be 200 metres to the south of a house. On the map the pictorial elements should have the same spatial relationship, only on a smaller scale. What the map and the real world have in common is the spatial relationship. So in terms of explanation some analogies may be 'true', in as much as the object under discussion has certain features, and to help explain this we refer to another object we are more familiar with, or which is simpler, but which has exactly the same feature. As long as the features are the same in both cases, the analogy might be termed 'true'. However, sometimes the analogy is used more poetically, just to help gain some form of understanding or to establish different ways of looking at the object.

Consider the simile of the sun. Part of the analogy compares the manner in which the Form of the good enables the possibility of knowledge to the way that the sun enables the possibility of sight. There seems to be a general pattern in both instances that x enables y. However, it is not clear that the analogy adds anything new here or even explains anything particularly well. Plato might as well simply have stated that the Form of the good enables knowledge. The pattern alluded to is so general that it does not really need a simile to make it clearer. If we look for more detail beyond this general pattern of x enabling y then the simile becomes a bit hazy. For example, the sun enables sight through the medium of light waves. Does the Form of the good enable knowledge through a medium too? The sunlight changes during the day; does the Form of the good also change in this way? Does Plato mean for these other patterns also to hold across the analogy, or do these elements merely add to the poetry of the simile?

Beyond being a mere tool for explanation, similes can help to expand our understanding of the world in new ways. Consider our scientific understanding of sound. Initially talk of 'sound waves' was just a metaphorical way of describing the spread of sound from a source, comparing it to the way waves ripple away from an object thrown in water. Later this idea was mathematically developed and the general idea of a wave as a means of transmitting a pattern through space emerged. This idea was later also applied to light. Here we have a comparison that started out as a simple poetical analogy and then developed into a scientific/mathematical model. The use of analogy has helped to extend the reach of science; indeed some claim it is possible to see the whole of science as the systemic development of metaphors.

More recently, the theory of evolution has started to be applied in many different contexts. It has even been applied to the way ideas and beliefs survive or disappear within the human world, with the term 'meme', a play on the word gene, being applied to ideas. Initially this may be a simile but may once again turn out to be a new development in social science. As with waves, it seems that the pattern ascribed by Darwin in the theory of evolution is a pattern that occurs elsewhere in the world.

So we can see that analogies have two roles in argument. One is to help explain a point; the other is to help clarify the nature of an object. In the first case, a pattern or feature of the object being discussed is explained by pointing out how this feature or element works in an object that is more familiar to the audience. However, we can see that sometimes what starts out as a way of simply making a point clearer actually helps to clarify the nature of the pattern or feature itself, which might then be mathematically applied in many different contexts.

Why does Plato use similes?

We should first note that the use of similes is not something that Plato alone is fond of. Similes are evident in the earliest examples of writing and are present in nearly every passage of writing since. In part this is because similes are embedded in our language. For example, consider the expression to 'grasp' an idea. This is a common-place expression, but it is a hidden simile. We are in effect saying something akin to 'I have firmly understood this idea', in the same way that I might firmly grasp an object in my hand. Interestingly it's also a very Platonic idea – treating ideas as if they were existing objects.

To see how embedded analogy is in our language, consider the small paragraph above. The terms *common-place*, *embedded*, *firmly* and *akin*, to name just a few, all seem to owe something to the use of simile or analogy. As did the word *owe* in the last sentence! It is impossible to escape use of analogy/simile in thought and language. This, it is argued, is because the ability to seek patterns in the world and the ability to compare objects with one another are some of the most basic, if not *the* most basic, human cognitive tools.

Traditionally metaphors are thought of as being incidental to language. In other words we have the literal use of language as the primary vehicle of communication and it just so happens that Plato chose this simile rather than another to illustrate his ideas. So nothing of philosophical significance hangs on Plato's decision to talk about the cave in comparing darkness to ignorance, and the sun in comparing light to the good.

However, the use of analogy is so common in human thought that it may be that it will always be an integral part of philosophical inquiry. If we view analogies in this way then the situation might be reversed. Plato's choice of simile may reflect ways of thinking entrenched in our languages so that we cannot help but think of ignorance as a kind of darkness, and the good as akin to light. In other words, it is no coincidence that Plato chose this simile, as our very understanding of goodness is inextricably bound up with analogies with light. This approach suggests that Plato's similes are not incidental pieces of detail designed to elaborate and illustrate his ideals, but reflect ways of thinking which systematically figure his philosophy and have continued to shape our thinking to this day. We cannot escape the simile of *light=good=knowledge* because that is how our thoughts have been formed. So the actual similes Plato used may be more important than we originally thought.

Returning to the cave

At 502c Plato began his explanation of the philosophical education of his rulers and through the three similes he has been elaborating the role of the Form of the good in that education. Now, using the simile of the cave, he expands on how education will produce good rulers and reinforces the important claim that it is a necessary condition of being a good ruler that one does not wish to rule.

Summary of the argument (517c–521b)

Read 517c–521b

- (517c–518d) Those who have left the cave will be unwilling to involve themselves once again in human affairs. If they return they will at first appear inept when involved in disputes with ordinary people about the *shadows* of justice. For the apprehension of the mind, like that of the eye, can be confused in two ways: one by coming from light into darkness and the other by coming from darkness into light. Education, as our account indicates, is not like a process of putting eyes into people who do not have them; it is a process of turning eyes in the right direction. The capacity to learn, and the organ with which to do it, are already present in everyone's soul, and so education is a skill of conversion by which people are turned from the world of change to that of being or reality.
- (518d–519b) While knowledge is innate, the other virtues (excellences) of the mind, like those of the body, must be implanted by training. People who are bad but clever employ their intelligence for bad purposes. If they had been well educated from childhood, the same capacity that is exercised on sensible objects would be directed instead toward the true realities.
- (519b–d) Rulers must not spend their whole lives being educated since they would refuse to act. But they must not be uneducated either since they would not have a single end at which to aim. The best natures must study so that they may see the good, and then they must return to the cave to rule.
- (519d–521b) Glaucon objects that we are doing the rulers an injustice by giving them a worse life when they might have a better. As before (420b), Socrates reminds Glaucon that the effort was not to give any one group within the

city a good life, but to gain advantage for the whole city by bringing its citizens into harmony and binding the city together. So it is just for the rulers to be compelled to rule. They will appreciate this when they realise that because they have been better educated than others they are able to have the life of ruler and philosopher. Only if the city is ruled by those who do not wish to rule but would rather be occupied with other things (namely, philosophy) will it be well ruled.

Interpretation and evaluation

This final passage is among the most important in the *Republic*, concerning the role of the rulers and their motivation to adopt it. Plato has already argued that the knowledge gained by doing philosophy is required of effective rulers. But here he makes the further point that philosophising is essential to ruling because it is *the* activity which is preferable to ruling; and rulers must prefer to do something other than rule if they are to rule well. For if they wanted to rule they would compete for the chance to do so and the city would be afflicted by strife (520d). The rulers' position is just, therefore, in virtue of their preference for doing something else. It is necessary that the philosopher suffer this *apparent* injustice in order for him and the city state to be truly just.

While it may be *just* for the philosophers to rule, the obvious question remains why they should be motivated to if they are personally better off philosophising. One argument at 520b suggests that the rulers will consent to rule because they appreciate that they should repay the city for their education. But this isn't the main argument. The answer is to be found in the nature of their acquaintance with objective good (504d–506a). People who apprehend the Form of the good itself will be motivated to realise what most closely approximates to the good in this world, namely the just state. Philosophers will not be motivated by personal benefit since it is only an apparent or relative good. To be governed by a single principle, that is to be motivated by the good, is to be reasonable; and to pursue one task is to be just. The unity of the philosophers' task lies in the fact that they are able to apprehend the good and devote themselves to trying to see it exemplified in the physical world. In this pursuit they avoid psychological conflict.

Socrates admits that the former prisoner, on his return to the cave, would appear to have no useful new knowledge and would be uninterested in politics. He would be clumsy at argument over the issues occupying the people around him.

Doesn't this suggest that knowledge of the good disqualifies the philosopher from government? Clearly for Plato it cannot. His point perhaps is that having seen reality the philosopher is no longer interested in contemporary or specifically *democratic* politics, with its concern for worldly honours and with the ability of the orator to cajole the crowd and play up to its whims. If he were allowed to dictate policy, however, his understanding of the good would enable him to aim directly at prudent policy and to see the shadows more keenly in virtue of having seen the originals.

However, there is a still a valid objection here. For in the cave we see that the cognitive world of the ordinary man is completely different from the philosopher's. The inside of the cave (as Plato has described it) bears little or no resemblance to the outside of the cave. So how can knowledge of the outside of the cave help to improve the lot of those who are forever stuck in the cave? Perhaps someone who is good at picking out the shadow on the wall should rule, or maybe someone who has looked at the fire and seen the puppets. This is a fairly big problem for Plato – sometimes he talks of the Forms as if they are somehow related to this world, and sometimes, as in the cave, he talks as if they are completely unrelated. The problem arises because Plato never gave a clear exposition of his theory of Forms, and so it is not clear how knowledge of the Forms might be applied to the physical.

Plato's theory of knowledge 2 – extended analysis

The sun, the line and the cave were all presented to help explain what knowledge of the good entails. In trying to answer this question Plato outlines an epistemology, i.e. a theory of knowledge. One important aspect of any theory of knowledge is to give an account of ultimate sources of knowledge.

Where does knowledge come from?

We all claim to know various facts about the world – the price of tomatoes, who wrote *Hamlet*, our birth dates, that 2 + 3 is 5. But where does this knowledge come from? Perhaps you learned about who wrote *Hamlet* from a teacher at school. But where did the teacher gain their knowledge? Perhaps they got it from a book. But this simply leads us to the further question of where the author of the book gained their knowledge. Perhaps from another book, which still leaves the question hanging. Ultimately this source must have come from someone who either knew Shakespeare or had seen copies of the original manuscript, or from Shakespeare himself who was well aware that he was the author. In either case the ultimate source of knowledge in this case was the senses: someone either seeing Shakespeare write the play (in the case of Shakespeare himself) or seeing the manuscript with this name on it.

Where does knowledge come from?

1 Copy the table below. Using the word 'know' in its everyday sense, write down four things that you know in the left-hand column.

2 Try to trace each piece of knowledge back to its ultimate source/origin.

3 Do the sources have anything in common? Does this reveal anything about the ultimate sources of knowledge?

Something that you know	The origin of this piece of knowledge
1	
2	
3	
4	

Traditionally philosophers have identified four ultimate sources of knowledge:

1 Reason
2 Experience
3 Revelation
4 Innate ideas.

■ Reason as the source of knowledge: rationalism

Rationalism is the view that the ultimate source of knowledge is reason. Rationalists often look to the world of mathematics as a template for their theory. Mathematical knowledge can be gained through reason alone and without the direct use of the senses. Alone in a room, cut off from the world, in theory it would be possible for me to work out substantial truths about geometric shapes and numbers just by thinking very hard. The mathematical knowledge that is gained in this way somehow appears to be eternal, or outside of time. In other words, while everything in the physical world comes in and out of existence, 2 + 3 will always be 5. Moreover mathematical knowledge seems to have a kind of certainty that exceeds other forms of knowledge. Knowledge that 2 + 3 = 5 appears unshakable, and it's difficult to see how one could be wrong about it. For these reasons, many rationalists thought that the model of mathematical knowledge, with its clarity and certainty, should be applied to all human knowledge. Through the application of reason, they argued, it would be possible to understand a significant body of knowledge about the world and how it operates. And this knowledge, like that of maths, would be certain, logical and endure for all time. The evidence of the senses should agree with the truths of reason but they are not required for the acquisition of these truths.

The idea that the rationalists embody is also reflected in literature and myth. It is encapsulated in the image of the wise hermit who withdraws from the world and contemplates the deep questions of life and the universe. Through the application of reason and thought alone the hermit slowly uncovers the essential truths about the world or the universal moral principles of life and so becomes exceedingly wise. The knowledge gained is not tainted by the ordinary concerns of everyday life and so has a kind of purity and eternity.

■ Experience as the source of knowledge: empiricism

Empiricism is the view that the ultimate source of knowledge is experience. Empiricists argue that we are born knowing nothing, with no 'innate' ideas. Everything we know, they claim, comes to us through our five senses. All our knowledge, indeed all our thoughts must ultimately be related to things we have seen, smelt, touched, tasted or heard.

The spirit of empiricism is also embodied in literature and myth. Here we encounter the character of the wise traveller: someone who has set out and explored the world, had many great and varied adventures and finally returns with the wisdom of experience.

■ Revelation as the source of knowledge: gnosticism

Another view of the origins of human knowledge claims that genuine wisdom is only to be gained by means of divine revelation. This view is sometimes called GNOSTICISM. Again we find this idea personified in myth and literature in the figure of the mystic: a wise and deeply spiritual person for whom special knowledge is given by some supernatural source and not through the senses or through reason.

■ Innate ideas as the source of knowledge

Some philosophers believe that we are born knowing certain things, in other words we are born with *innate* knowledge. Is this true? It is undeniable that we are born with certain instincts: to suckle, to cry when hungry, etc. However, whether these count as knowledge is debatable. After all, do swallows *know* that they must fly south in autumn? Do squirrels *know* that the winter is coming and so they should store nuts? It seems likely that they have no explicit understanding of these facts, but simply act instinctively. However, believers in innate knowledge argue that beyond instinct certain other elements, such as a moral sense, or a knowledge of God or of abstract principles or of mathematics, may also be known innately. The belief in innate knowledge is traditionally associated with rationalism, since rationalists often felt that reason revealed knowledge buried within our minds that we were born with.

ACTIVITY   Which of the above four explanations, either alone or in combination, best describes the position of Plato?

One obvious answer emerging from the *Republic*, in particular from the simile of the line, is that Plato believed the ultimate source of knowledge was reason; in other words, Plato was a rationalist. In the simile of the line we see a clear division between the physical world on the one hand and the world of ideas on the other and a corresponding distinction between belief and reason. One of the key points is that from the physical world we can derive only beliefs; knowledge must come from the world of ideas. This is a clear rejection of empiricism – the belief that *all* knowledge must come from the senses. For Plato *no* knowledge can come from the senses, only beliefs can. Also, the status accorded to maths in the simile suggests that knowledge of the Forms will be obtained by a rational process of thought; again this would seem to place Plato firmly in the rationalist camp.

However, the simile of the cave introduces a mystical element into this picture. The prisoner is mysteriously freed, has an urge to go upwards, where he 'beholds' the truth. In many ways this could be a simile for knowledge as divine revelation; that is, gnosticism.

■ What will gaining knowledge feel like?

This will depend on your interpretation of Plato's theory of Forms. If you adopt the standard interpretation then knowledge will be like an apprehension of something, an intelligible object that exists outside yourself. Perhaps this apprehension feels like a 'eureka' moment? Plato does not shed much light on this question. If, however, you adopt the alternative 'secular' interpretation, then gaining knowledge will be like working out the perfect set of concepts, perfect in relation to the good – this presumably will be more akin to mathematics, where logical reasoning is accompanied by the final sense of grasping something.

On either account we must remember that by 'knowledge' Plato means something different from how we use it today (see pages 87–8 for more on the differences). We use the word to cover many types of beliefs, about history, about the world around us. Plato seems to be reserving the word for a very special class of cases. By 'knowledge' he means our grasp of eternal truths – truths that are not bound up in time in the way that historical facts are. Plato means such things as mathematics, the nature of beauty, the good. In his view these things are eternal and cannot be derived from the ever-changing world in which we live. The answers somehow sit above this world. It is because of this that Plato is considered a rationalist, believing that eternal truths cannot be gained through the senses. The senses only reveal the changing world around us. Plato's account of knowledge seems more akin to how we might ascribe the term wisdom.

Because Plato thought that the good was the ultimate source of all knowledge, it follows that knowledge has a moral dimension for Plato. In other words if you know what is good you will automatically act to achieve it. Plato, following Socrates, claimed that all human actions are aimed at what humans believe to be good for them. Unfortunately most humans do not actually know what is genuinely good for them (as they do not know the Form of the good). But if humans did have knowledge of the good they would be able to aim for what is genuinely good and thus live a good life. In this way, knowledge is virtue according to Plato, a virtue being any quality that enables you to bring about good.

What counts as knowledge, how it is defined and where it comes from are still live philosophical questions. Plato's theory of knowledge was the first attempt to answer some of these questions so we should expect the theory to be a bit patchy by today's standards. Below we have summarised some of the strengths and weaknesses of Plato's theory of knowledge.

Strengths of Plato's theory of knowledge

- ◼ It recognises that knowledge is largely conceptual
Plato suggests that knowledge consists of grasping ideas, and to some extent this is surely right. Without any ideas or concepts all life would be pretty meaningless, just an endless flow of colours and noises. It is humans' ability to classify these sensations into types or perhaps 'Forms' that enables us

to generalise and make claims about the world. We live in a world of physical objects, but it is our ability to think about more than the objects immediately in front of us that makes knowledge possible. In this sense Plato is right that knowledge must involve the intelligible realm, although his claim that it is *purely* derived from the intelligible realm is less plausible.

■ It rejects rhetoric

Plato's insistence on reason as the means to the truth may seem obvious. However, this must be viewed against a background where rhetoric was the dominant mode of persuasion. Even today, with religion as popular as ever and advertising affecting our spending and habits, does reason really govern our decision making? The insistence of Socrates and Plato on reason as the means to the truth is a significant turning point in western culture, although some commentators have claimed that western society is now too rational or 'logo-centric' and would be better if it were slightly more, say, mystical.

■ It is in tune with the way that many people think

Many people talk as if concepts are somehow out there and independent of humans. People often speak about justice being done as if there exists an objective 'thing', justice, that exists independently of humans and either appears in a situation or not. The same is true of the way many people talk about love. Talking about concepts or ideas as if they exist is often referred to as being '*platonic*' about ideas. So it is true that Plato's theory of ideas is reflected in our language and to some extent in the way we think about some important concepts.

■ It shows how values could be objective

On pages 15–16 we examined the sophists' claim that there are no objective truths concerning values or taste, and that such issues are simply a matter of opinion. Such relativism has led some to argue that all areas of thought, including science, are simply matters of opinion and that objective truth is impossible. Relativism about morals can be difficult to argue against, other than to claim that God exists and so decrees a set of objective values. Plato's theory of Forms and his subsequent epistemology sketches out a position that can counter relativism. Perhaps, as Plato suggests, there *is* a perfect set of concepts. It is certainly true of science, and perhaps true of other areas of human inquiry, that our concepts seem to be better at describing the world than they used to be. Hundreds of years ago our scientific concepts were very different and not very useful in terms of making inventions and manipulating the world. Science seems to be making progress. One day the concepts used in science might map the world exactly and the same might happen in other areas of thought. The idea of a perfect set of concepts is an appealing one, which offers a riposte to the relativist.

Plato's claim is not, however, based on scientific progress, which is founded on observation. For Plato, it is the moral concept of the good that will enable us to derive a perfect set of concepts and this will be reached through pure reason.

Criticisms of Plato's theory of knowledge

■ He derives the epistemology from the ontology

Plato first puts forward a belief that, as well as the physical world which we observe with the senses, there exists a world of ideal 'Forms' perceived by the mind. He then proceeds to define knowledge in terms of these Forms, as genuine knowledge involves apprehension of them. In so doing Plato is deriving his epistemology (his theory of knowledge) from his ontology (his theory of reality) and this, according to many people, is the wrong way to go about things. The objection is that only once you have put forward a theory of knowledge should you start to make claims about the sort of things that exist in the world. This way your claims about the world can be validated by your theory of knowledge. Descartes was the first philosopher to make this move (putting his epistemology first), and is often regarded as definitive of the 'modern' era in philosophy.

■ It is elitist

In Plato's view, knowledge is only accessible by a few people, the true philosophers; and this can be accused of elitism. His view also seems to go against our everyday conception, whereby most people would claim to know quite a few things. Admittedly, some knowledge, for example the theory of relativity, is not easily grasped by most. And in the dark ages when literacy in Europe was minimal, it is also true to say that a great deal of knowledge was retained by only a few scholars. However, today, with high literacy rates, universal education and the rise of the Internet, we have seen a massive spread or 'democratisation' of knowledge. Just by sitting at a computer and running a few searches you can find out the answer to most questions.

This analysis of course relies on a different concept of knowledge from that used by Plato and it is certainly not easy to type a few words into a computer and come out with a definitive definition of the good. However, the idea that only a few people can glimpse the truth, and further that these people should rule in our best interest, is certainly anti-democratic.

■ It is dangerous

Believing there are objective values might be appealing when considering issues such as morality or justice. However, is it helpful to believe that beauty or taste is objective? Can't one person's preference in music simply be different from another person's rather than better or worse? Is everything to be measured against an 'objective' yardstick? This idea that all values admit of objective answers is dangerous if it leads to intolerance, with people insisting that their ideas are definitely right, rather than acknowledging that certain areas only admit of opinion.

■ It does not account for scientific progress

Plato's vision of knowledge was very different from that of his protégé Aristotle. Whereas Plato thought that knowledge could be gained through reason alone, Aristotle believed that knowledge could be gained through observing and classifying the world. In relation to the massive growth of science in the last few hundred years, it is clear that Aristotle's model is a more accurate account. Although reason is also involved, science is primarily founded on experimentation. It is impossible, using reason alone, to work out what the world must be like.

However, when explaining different aspects of the world we often choose idealised models. In a biology textbook you might see an outline of a human body with only the heart, lungs and veins showing the human circulation system. Here it will not be a specific person's circulation that is shown, but rather an abstract/idealised version, what you might call the 'Form' of human circulation. Again, a generic picture of a 'cell' will be familiar to most school students. Such idealised versions are common in teaching and help us to understand the world. However, the model of a cell is only attained by studying hundreds and thousands of different cells, in other words by using the senses, and not, as Plato claimed was possible, by simply arguing or discussing what a cell must be like, devoid of the senses.

Once again though, this criticism does not apply when we look into the moral realm. Here it seems it is not the case that we can derive moral truths from observation. Abstract discussion and dialogue seems to be the preferred method.

In relation to science, presumably Plato is committed to the view that all Forms already exist and that new Forms don't appear overnight. If this is the case, then the Form of the perfect dishwasher or television must have existed back in Plato's day. Perhaps these advanced Forms are what scientists stumble upon when they have a Eureka moment and come up with a new invention!

■ It suggests knowledge is defined by its object

As discussed earlier on page 148, the idea of distinguishing knowledge from opinion on the basis of the different kinds of objects the mind deals with seems a little alien in today's world. Nowadays we tend to think that knowledge and belief can be about the same kinds of object, the two categories being separated by the degrees of evidence required in each case.

■ It is unclear what gaining knowledge will be like

Although it may be argued that Plato's *Republic* outlines the Form of the perfect city and attempts to give an account of the Form of justice, Socrates does not claim to have knowledge of any of the Forms and admits his radical ignorance of the Form of the good. With the lack of a clear example of knowledge, it remains unclear what gaining knowledge involves or will feel like. Perhaps accompanying the grasping of a Form there is a feeling of rightness? However, if this is a subjective feeling then how can one be sure that the feeling is correct and not just triggered by, say, a chemical imbalance in the brain? And are the public simply to take the philosopher's word for it that they have gained knowledge of the Forms purely based on a subjective feeling of rightness? Without clarity on the issue of apprehending a Form, Plato's theory of knowledge remains rather vague.

Key points: Chapter 8

What you need to know about the **simile of the cave**:

1 Plato represents the human epistemic condition and the development of the philosopher by outlining a simile involving prisoners in a cave looking at shadows on a wall. One of the prisoners, representing the philosopher, is freed and sees the shapes that cause the shadows. He then travels further and beholds real objects in the world outside the cave.

2 The simile represents the philosophers leaving behind the world of the senses and achieving an understanding of the truth through an apprehension of the Forms.

3 The simile of the cave provides a more poetical account of Plato's theory of knowledge than the account provided in the preceding simile of the line. However, it is not altogether clear that the accounts match completely. The question of what Plato considers to be the normal human state of knowledge, or rather of opinion, seems to be different in the two similes.

4 Although using similes can be an effective and legitimate method of reasoning we should be wary of reading too much into them.

5 The account of knowledge emerging from the similes of the line and cave is very different from the way we use the concept in modern society and is open to several criticisms.

6 Philosophers who have knowledge of the good will be motivated to rule, not by personal benefit, but because they can help bring about the just state and so replicate the Form of the good.

Glossary

ANTITHESIS   A contrary, often opposite set of ideas to a **thesis**.

ARGUMENTATION   A sequence or exchange of arguments on a particular topic.

CONSEQUENTIALIST ETHICS   A type of moral theory which views the moral value of an action to lie in its consequences. So an action is judged to be good if it brings about beneficial consequences, and bad if it brings about harmful ones. This is in contrast to **deontological ethics**.

CONTINGENT TRUTH   A truth that is logically possible to be false. For example, 'Tony Blair was Prime Minister in 2006' is true, but he might not have been. Unlike **necessary truths**, contingent truths could have been otherwise.

COUNTER-EXAMPLE   When someone proposes a definition or theory concerning a particular topic, a counter-example shows an instance in which that definition or theory does not work. For example, if I claimed that only men were likely to be elected as Prime Minister of the UK, someone might cite Margaret Thatcher as a counter-example.

DEMOCRACY   Power or force of the people, from the Greek *demos* meaning people and *kratos* meaning power or force. In Athens this 'rule by the power of the people' entailed every citizen being entitled to attend assembly meetings and vote on the issues of the day.

DEONTOLOGICAL ETHICS   A type of moral theory which views the moral value of an action to lie in the action itself. So an action is right or wrong in itself, whatever the consequences. Generally deontologists (such as Kant) proposed certain principles that guide us to which actions are right and which are wrong. This is in contrast to **consequentialist ethics**.

DESCRIPTIVE   A descriptive statement is one that describes the world as it is. It contains only factual claims, as opposed to a **prescriptive** statement which claims how the world should be.

DIALECTIC   A way of arguing using logic to discuss and analyse differing opinions on a topic. Often associated with the sequence of **thesis, antithesis** and **synthesis**.

DUTY   An action which we are required or impelled to carry out.

EMPIRICAL   Of or relating to experience. Empirical knowledge is knowledge gained through experience or experiment, in other words through the senses.

EPISTEMOLOGY   The theory of knowledge; the study of what is to count as knowledge, from the Greek *episteme* meaning knowledge and *logos* meaning account or rationale.

EXISTENTIAL   Of or relating to existence.

GNOSTICISM   The theory that the true source of knowledge is divine revelation.

GOOD   By the term 'good' Plato means that which we all seek. Everyone has their own conception, however vague, of what is good for them and most spend their life trying to achieve this good, be it accruing money, seeking experience or chasing pleasure, etc. Plato believed however that there was a singular conception of the good that could only be achieved through philosophy; in other words by grasping the form of the good.

HEDONISM   The theory that pleasure is the only good worth pursuing.

HYPOTHESIS   An idea put forward as a potential solution to a problem or query.

INFINITE REGRESS   A regress is a process of reasoning from effect to cause or of going backwards in a chain of explanation. An infinite regress is one where the process never stops, where it is repeated endlessly. This is generally considered problematic in a philosophical argument, and a sign that a mistake has been made.

METAPHYSICS The area of philosophy concerned with what the world is really and truly like. For example, the debate about free will versus determinism is a metaphysical debate, because it seeks to find out whether or not humans are ultimately free or determined by the laws of nature.

MIMETIC See MIMESIS.

MIMESIS Representation of the world or ideas through art, from the Greek for imitation/ representation. Art that attempts to imitate the world is called *mimetic* art. Plato claimed that physical objects are imitations of the ideal forms. Art in turn is an imitation of physical objects and so is twice removed from the reality of the forms. In this way Plato was very sceptical about what could be learnt from art, in particular from poetry.

MORAL RELATIVISM This is the view that moral judgements vary according to the social context in which they are made. So moral values or standards of conduct are different in different societies: what is right for you may not be right for me, etc.

NECESSARY TRUTH A truth which has to be true and couldn't be otherwise, or for which it is logically impossible that it be false. For example, 'a triangle has three sides' is a necessary truth as it is logically impossible for a triangle to have two sides.

OBJECTIVISM The claim that value judgements and aesthetic judgements can be true; in other words that morality and aesthetics are not just matters of opinion but can be matters of fact.

OLIGARCHY Rule by the few, from the Greek *oligon* meaning few and *arkho* meaning rule. An oligarchy is where the power lies with a few people or families, often the wealthy.

ONTOLOGY The study of being in general, in other words the attempt to give a theory about what exists.

PARADIGMS A particular way or related set of ways of viewing the world or a way of approaching an activity.

PLURALIST A society consisting of people with differing values and beliefs.

PREDICATIVE A sentence that asserts that an object or event has a particular quality e.g. redness.

PRESCRIPTIVE A prescriptive statement prescribes how the world should be, as opposed to a **descriptive** sentence which states how the world is. Prescriptive statements are usually moral claims.

PRE-SOCRATICS A term used to describe all the Greek philosophers prior to the period when Socrates was active.

PSYCHIC HARMONY Plato claims that psychic harmony is achieved when the three parts of the soul are appropriately balanced, with reason controlling the appetites (desires) and the spirit (will).

RATIONALISM The theory that the true source of knowledge is reason, as opposed to **empiricism** which claims that the true source of knowledge is the senses.

RIGHTS Entitlements that I have to the protection of certain powers, interests or privileges. It is debatable whether we can have rights only because we make a contract within society, or whether we have 'natural rights' which exist independently of any contract. Rights may be seen as the converse of duties; so if I have a right to X then others have a **duty** to promote X or at least not interfere in my access to X.

SENSE EXPERIENCE All of the sensations that we gain through the senses, in other words all of the colours, smells, tastes, etc. that form a large part of our conscious experience.

SOPHISTS The Sophists were a group of unrelated philosophers/teachers/speakers. Most sophists would travel from city to city, often accompanied by young wealthy men whose parents were paying for the educational experience, and give talks to a paying public.

SUPERSENSIBLE Beyond the senses.

SYNTHESIS A merging of ideas between two conflicting viewpoints (usually a **thesis** and an **antithesis**).

THEORY OF FORMS The name given to Plato's theory that ideas or concepts such as that of beauty have some type of existence independent of human minds. Such ideas or concepts have been labelled as Forms. Plato believed that true knowledge can only be gained by grasping these Forms. The theory of Forms is also sometimes called the theory of ideas.

THESIS An idea or related set of ideas concerning a particular issue.

THIRD MAN ARGUMENT An argument put forward by Plato's pupil Aristotle that criticises Plato's theory of Forms. The exact formulation of the third man argument is somewhat disputed, however the criticism runs something along these lines. The theory of Forms serves to explain how different objects can partake of a particular quality by suggesting that they resemble a particular Form. In other words all beautiful objects are beautiful in virtue of the fact that they resemble the Form of beauty. However if we need an extra element (the Form) to explain what unites all objects that partake of a quality then introducing an extra element would imply that we need yet another third element. For what is it that the beautiful objects and the Form of beauty all have in common? Presumably this would need to be explained by the resemblance to a third object, something like the Form of the Form of beauty, and so on. Aristotle is suggesting that the theory of Forms can lead to an **infinite regress**.

TIMARCHY/TIMOCRACY A government rules through the strength of the principle of honour in its people.

TOTALITARIANISM When a government controls almost every aspect of an individual's life.

TWO-WORLD VIEW The idea that there are two separate realms of existence. For Plato these realms consist of the physical world as revealed by our senses and the world of Forms as revealed by reason.

TYRANNY When one person gains absolute power.

UNIVERSALS General terms for types or properties; for example, 'redness' or 'dog'.

UTILITARIANISM The moral theory based around the idea that a good act is one that increases general happiness and a bad act is one that decreases general happiness or causes pain.

VALUE JUDGEMENT A value judgement is a decision about the rightness or goodness of something. For example, believing that abortion is wrong would be a value judgement.

VERIDICAL Truthful, in line with the truth.

VIRTUES Character traits or dispositions which are to be valued. Common virtues include wisdom, courage, self-control, honesty, generosity. For Plato a virtue was a character trait that enables the individual to achieve the good.

Notes

1 Desmond Lee in his translator's introduction to the *Republic*, Penguin Classics 2003, p. 56.

2 This paradox was not 'solved' until over 2000 years later when Isaac Newton and the philosopher Leibniz simultaneously invented calculus, which shows that the sum of a series of infinitesimal numbers can add up to a whole integer.

3 This idea is taken from J. Hayward, G. Jones and M. Mason, *Exploring Ethics*, Hodder Murray 2000.

4 It is interesting to note that other forms of government, such as monarchy, anarchy, oligarchy, have the 'archy' suffix – deriving from the Greek term 'to rule'. Democracy on the other hand has a 'cracy' ending deriving from the Greek for power or force. In theory 'rule by the people' should be termed demo*archy*. Demo*cracy* translates as 'force or power of the people'. Some suggest that this term 'democracy' was deliberately coined by critics of the system who wanted to emphasise the brutish mob element and play down its ability to rule effectively.

5 Simonides was a famous Greek poet.

6 Note that this is in no way connected with anything Simonides ever actually wrote.

7 Polemarchus cannot consistently maintain the positions put forward in lines 111 and 119 of Book 1 because they can contradict each other: it appears to be both just and unjust to harm men that we think are bad (but are in fact good).

8 We have seen that sophists, like Thrasymachus, used to charge for their instruction.

9 For more on the distinction between deontological and consequentialist theories of ethics see Chapter 2 of D. Cardinal, G. Jones and J. Hayward, *Moral Philosophy: A Guide to Ethical Theory*, Hodder Murray 2006.

10 Nearly two thousand years after the *Republic* this type of social contract theory was revived by political philosophers such as Thomas Hobbes and John Locke.

11 J. R. R. Tolkien, *The Fellowship of the Ring*, Harper Collins 1993, pp. 517–18.

12 Julia Annas, *An Introduction to Plato's Republic*, Oxford University Press, 1981, p. 73.

13 Aldous Huxley, *Brave New World*, Penguin 1959, p. 33.

14 Annas, *An Introduction to Plato's Republic*, p. 137.

15 In the 1990s the divided soul was brought into American living rooms through the TV sitcom *Herman's Head*. Herman was a man who was driven by conflicting drives in his head, each drive represented by a different actor (a sensitive woman, a lusty fratboy, an anxious wimp, and an intellectual genius). The comic *Beano* also updated Plato's divided soul for kids in 'The Numskulls'.

16 Huxley, *Brave New World*, p. 42.

17 Annas, *An Introduction to Plato's Republic*, pp. 182–3.

18 Following the Penguin translation, we translate *doxa* as 'opinion'.

19 Plato also had a personal axe to grind in referring to the sight lovers. The Academy offered an education based on mathematics, philosophy and reasoning; the Socratic dialogues, including the *Republic*, were used as training materials. However, this form of education, which would not look out of place today, was unusual in its time. The standard education at the time (only the wealthy, of course, were educated) was to travel around, usually with an older mentor or sophist, and take in lots of sights and experiences. So Plato is keen to show in this passage that his method of education is far superior, for only his method can ever produce true knowledge; merely travelling and seeing sights can only ever produce beliefs.

20 Odysseus tells his captor Polyphemus, the Cyclops, that his name is 'noman' and so, when Odysseus blinds the Cyclops and makes his getaway, and Polyphemus calls to his neighbours for help 'My friends, noman

is killing me by sleight', no one comes to his aid, supposing that his trouble is 'some unavoidable malady'. *Odyssey*, Book 9.

21 For a more detailed analysis of this interpretation see Annas, *An Introduction to Plato's Republic*, pp. 197ff.

22 The basic idea, attributable to Hume, is that it is impossible to derive an *ought* from an *is*, in other words, that we cannot reason validly from premises involving only factual premises to conclusions about what ought to be done.

Selected bibliography

Annas, J., *An Introduction to Plato's Republic*,
Oxford: OUP 1981.

Melling, D., *Understanding Plato*, Oxford: OUP
1987.

Pappas, N., *Plato and the Republic*, London:
Routledge 1995.

Robinson, D., *Introducing Plato*, Cambridge:
Icon 2000.

Russell, B., *History of Western Philosophy*, New
York: Simon & Schuster 1946.

White, N., *A Companion to Plato's Republic*,
Oxford: Blackwell 1979.

Index

Philosophy in Focus

Epistemology: The
Theory of Knowledge
978 07195 79677

Philosophy of Religion
978 07195 79684

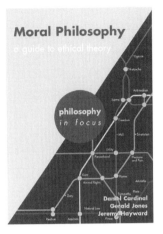

Moral Philosophy
978 0340 888056

Existentialism and
Humanism:
Jean-Paul Sartre
978 07195 71886

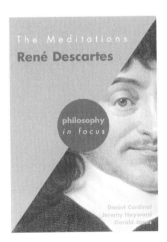

The Meditations:
René Descartes
978 0340 888049

The Republic:
Plato
978 0340 888032